AFRICAN SCHOLAR PUBLICATIONS
www.lulu.com/egipt

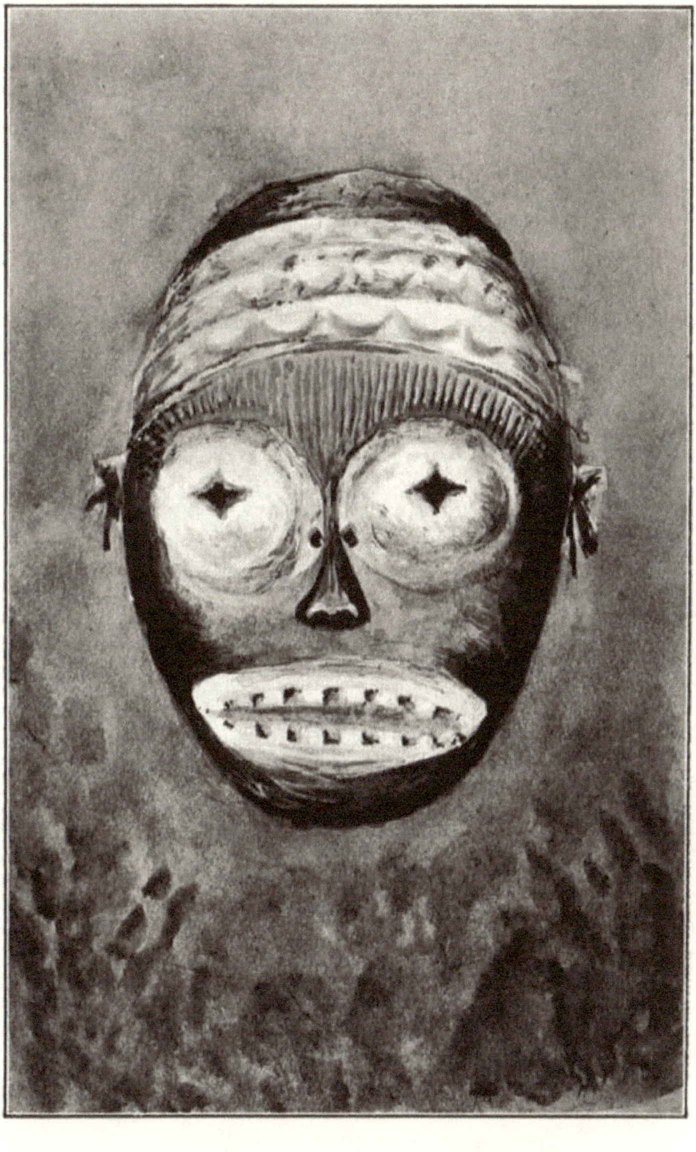

JU-JU MASK FROM IBO COUNTRY, SOUTHERN NIGERIA

AFRICAN SCHOLAR PUBLICATIONS
www.lulu.com/egipt

FOLK STORIES

FROM

SOUTHERN NIGERIA
WEST AFRICA

BY

ELPHINSTONE DAYRELL, F.R.G.S., F.R.A.I.

DISTRICT COMMISSIONER, SOUTHERN NIGERIA

Re-published by African Scholar Publications 2016.

Edited by Faheem Judah-EL

WITH AN INTRODUCTION BY

ANDREW LANG

WITH FRONTISPIECE

LONGMANS, GREEN AND CO.

39 PATERNOSTER ROW, LONDON

NEW YORK, BOMBAY, AND CALCUTTA

1910

AFRICAN SCHOLAR PUBLICATIONS
www.lulu.com/egipt

ABOUT THE EDITOR

FAHEEM JUDAH-EL

Born on September 15th 1962 in Decatur Illinois:

Faheem Judah-El is a Researcher and Historian: He has spent many years chronicling and preserving the story of African people worldwide. As a researcher He has traveled to many parts of the world such as: Ethiopia, Egypt, Mecca, Mexico, Kenya, South Africa, Uganda and many Native American Mound Centers of North America. He is currently an author, and the Editor of African Scholar Publications & Preservation.

ISBN 978-1-329-80714-3

AFRICAN SCHOLAR PUBLICATIONS
www.lulu.com/egipt

CONTENTS

Frontispiece from a Drawing in Colour by
Major G. M. DE L. DAYRELL

lives in the Water

[vii]

INTRODUCTION

Many years ago a book on the Folk-Tales of the Eskimo was published, and the editor of *The Academy* (Dr. Appleton) told one of his minions to send it to me for revision. By mischance it was sent to an eminent expert in Political Economy, who, never suspecting any error, took the book for the text of an interesting essay on the economics of "the blameless Hyperboreans."

Mr. Dayrell's "Folk Stories from Southern Nigeria" appeal to the anthropologist within me, no less than to the lover of what children and older people call "Fairy Tales." The stories are full of mentions of strange institutions, as well as of rare adventures. I may be permitted to offer some running notes and comments on this mass of African curiosities from the crowded lumber-room of the native mind.

I. *The Tortoise with a Pretty Daughter.*—The story, like the tales of the dark native tribes of Australia, rises from that state of fancy by which man draws (at least for purposes of fiction) no line between himself and the lower animals. Why should not the fair heroine, Adet, daughter of the tortoise, be the daughter of human parents? The tale would be none the less interesting, and a good deal more credible to the mature intelligence. But the ancient[viii] fashion of animal parentage is presented. It may have originated, like the stories of the Australians, at a time when men were totemists, when every person had a bestial or vegetable "family-name," and when, to account for these hereditary names, stories of descent from a supernatural, bestial, primeval race were invented. In the fables of the world, speaking animals, human in all but outward aspect, are the characters. The fashion is universal among savages; it descends to the Buddha's *jataka*, or parables, to Æsop and La Fontaine. There could be no such fashion if fables had originated among civilised human beings.

The polity of the people who tell this story seems to be despotic. The king makes a law that any girl prettier than the prince's fifty wives shall be put to death, with her parents. Who is to be the Paris, and give the fatal apple to the most fair? Obviously the prince is the Paris. He falls in love with Miss Tortoise, guided to her as he is by the bird who is "entranced with her beauty." In this tribe, as in Homer's time, the lover offers a bride-price to the father of the girl. In Homer cattle are the current medium; in Nigeria pieces of cloth and brass rods are (or were) the currency. Observe the queen's interest in an affair of true love. Though she knows that her son's life is endangered by his honourable passion, she adds to the bride-price out of her privy purse. It is "a long courting"; four years pass, while pretty Adet is "ower young to marry yet." The king is very angry when the news of this breach of the royal marriage Act first comes to his ears. He summons the whole of his subjects, his throne, a[ix]stone, is set out in the market-place, and Adet is brought before him. He sees and is conquered.

"It is no wonder," said the king, "This tortoise-girl might be a queen."

Though a despot, his Majesty, before cancelling his law, has to consult the eight Egbos, or heads of secret societies, whose magical powers give the sacred sanction to legislation. The Egbo (see p. 4, note) is a mumbo-jumbo man. He answers to the bogey who presides over the rites of initiation in the Australian tribes.

When the Egbo is about, women must hide and keep out of the way. The king proclaims the cancelling of the law. The Egbos might resist, for they have all the knives and poisons of the secret societies behind them. But the king, a master of the human heart, acts like Sir Robert Walpole. He buys the Egbo votes "with palm-wine and money," and gives a feast to the women at the marriage dances. But why does the king give half his kingdom to the tortoise? When an adventurer in fairy tales wins the hand of the king's heiress, he usually gets half the kingdom. The tortoise is said to have been "the wisest of all men and animals." Why? He merely did not kill his daughter. But there is no temptation to kill daughters in a country where they are valuable assets, and command high bride-prices. In the Australian tribes, the bride-price is simply another girl. A man swops his sister to another man for the other man's sister, or for any girl of whose hand the other man has the disposal.[x]

II. The second story is a very ingenious commercial parable, "Never lend money, you only make a dangerous enemy." The story also explains why bush cats eat poultry.

III. *The Woman with Two Skins* is a peculiar version of the story of the courteous Sir Gawain with his bride, hideous by day, and a pearl of loveliness by night. The Ju Ju man answers to the witch in our fairy tales and to the mother-in-law of the prince, who, by a magical potion, makes him forget his own true love. She, however, is always victorious, and the prince

"Prepares another marriage, Their hearts so full of love and glee,"

and ousts the false bride, like Lord Bateman in the ballad, when Sophia came home. In this case of Lord Bateman, the scholiast (Thackeray, probably) suggests that his

8

Lordship secured the consent of the Church as the king in the tortoise story won that of the Egbos. Our tale then wanders into the fairy tale of the king who is deceived into drowning his children, in European folk-lore, because he is informed that they are puppies. The Water Ju Ju, however, saves these black princes, and brings forward the rightful heir very dramatically at a wrestling match, where the lad overthrows more than he thought, like Orlando in *As You Like It*, and conquers the heart of the jealous queen as well as his athletic opponents.

In the conclusion the jealous woman is handed over to the ecclesiastical arm of the Egbos; she is flogged, and, as in the case of Jeanne d'Arc, is[xi] burned alive, "and her ashes were thrown into the river." Human nature is much the same everywhere.

IV. *The King's Magic Drum.*—The drum is the mystic cauldron of ancient Welsh romance, which "always provides plenty of good food and drink." But the drum has its drawback, the food "goes bad" if its owner steps over a stick in the road or a fallen tree, a tabu like the *geisas* of ancient Irish legends. The tortoise, in this tale, has the *geisas* power; he can make the king give him anything he chooses to ask. This very queer constraint occurs constantly in the Cuchullain cycle of Irish romances, and in *The Black Thief.* (You can buy it for a penny in Dublin, or read it in Thackeray's *Little Tour in Ireland.*) The King is constrained to part with the drum, but does not tell the tortoise about the tabu and the drawback. The tortoise, though disappointed, at least pays his score off in public, and then the tale wanders into the *Hop o' my Thumb* formula, and the trail of ashes. Finally the story, like most stories, explains the origin of an animal peculiarity, why tortoises live under prickly tie-tie palms. That explanation was clearly in the author's mind from the first, but to reach his point he adopted the formula of the mystic object, drum or cauldron, which provides endless supplies, and has a counteracting charm attached to it, a tabu.

V. *Ituen and the King's Wife.*—Some of these tales have this peculiarity, that the characters possess names, as Ituen, Offiong, and Attem. They are thus what people call *sagas*, not mere *Märchen*. All the pseudo-historic legends of the Greek states, of Thebes,[xii] Athens, Mycenæ, Pylos, and so on, are folk-tales converted into saga, and adapted and accepted as historical. Some of these Nigerian fairy-tales are in the same cast. The story of Athamas of Iolcos and the sacrifice of any of his descendants who went into the town hall, exactly corresponds to the fate of the family of Ituen (p. 32).[1] The whole Athamas story, in Greece, is a tissue of popular tales found in every part of the world. This Ituen story, as usual, explains the habits of animals, vultures, and dogs, and illustrates the awful cruelties of Egbo law.

VI. *The Pretty Stranger* is a native variant of *Judith and Holofernes.*

VII. A "Just So Story," a myth to explain the ways of animals. The cauldron of Medea, which destroyed the wrong old person, and did not rejuvenate him, is introduced. "All the stories have been told," all the world over.

VIII. *The Disobedient Daughter who Married a Skull.*—This is most original; though all our ballads and tales about the pretty girl who is carried to the land of the dead by her lover's ghost (Bürger's *Lenore*) have the same fundamental idea. Then comes in the common moral, the Reward of Courtesy, as in Perrault's *Les Fées*. But the machinery of the Nigerian romance leads up to the Return of Proserpine from the Dead in a truly fanciful way.

IX. *The King who Married the Cock's Daughter* is Æsop's man who married the woman that had been a cat. As Adia unen pecks at the corn, the other lady caught and ate a mouse.

[xiii]

X. *The Woman, the Ape, and the Child.*—This tale illustrates Egbo juridicature very powerfully, and is told to account for Nigerian marriage law.

XI. *The Fish and the Leopard's Wife.*—Another "Just So Story."

XII. *The Bat.*—Another explanation of the nocturnal habits of the bat. The tortoise appears as the wisest of things, like the hare in North America, Brer Rabbit, the Bushman Mantis insect, and so on.

XIII., XIV., XV. All of these are explanatory "Just So Stories."

XVI. *Why the Sun and Moon live in the Sky.*—Sun and Moon, in savage myth, lived on earth at first, but the Nigerian explanation of their retreat to the sky is, as far as I know, without parallel elsewhere.

XVII., XVIII. "Just So Stories."

XIX. Quite an original myth of Thunder and Lightning: much below the divine dignity of such myths elsewhere. Thunder is not the Voice of Zeus or of Baiame the Father (Australian), but of an old sheep! The gods have not made the Nigerians poetical.

XX. Another "Just So Story."

XXI. *The Cock who caused a Fight* illustrates private war and justice among the natives, and shows the Egbos refusing to admit the principle of a fine in atonement for an offence.

XXII. *The Affair of the Hippopotamus and of the Tortoise.*—A very curious variant of the *Whuppitie Stoorie*, or Tom-Tit-Tot story, depending on the power conferred by learning the secret name of an opponent. These secret names are conferred at Australian ceremonies. Any amount of the learning about secret names is easily accessible.[xiv]

XXIII. *Why Dead People are Buried.*—Here we meet the Creator so common in the religious beliefs of Africans as of most barbarous and savage peoples. "The Creator was a big chief." The Euahlayi Baiame is rendered "Big Man" by Mrs. Langloh Parker (see The *Euahlayi Tribe*). The myth is one of world-wide diffusion, explaining The Origin of Death, usually by the fable of a message, forgotten and misrendered, from the Creator.

XXIV. *The Fat Woman who Melted Away.*—The revival of this beautiful creature, from all that was left of her, the toe, is an incident very common in folk-tales, i.e. the Scottish *Rashin Coatie*. (The word "dowry" is used throughout where "bride-price" would better express the institution. The Homeric ἕνα is meant.)

XXV. *The Leopard, the Squirrel, and the Tortoise.*—A "Just So Story."

XXVI. *Why the Moon Waxes and Wanes.*—A lunar myth; not a poetical though a kindly explanation of the habits of the moon.

XXVII. *The Story of the Leopard, the Tortoise, and the Bush Rat.*—A "Just So Story."

XXVIII. *The King and the JuJu Tree.*—This is a fine example of Ju Ju beliefs, and of an extraordinary sacrifice to a Ju Ju power located in a tree. Goats, chickens, and white men are common offerings, but "seven baskets of flies" might propitiate Beelzebub. The "spirit-man" who can succeed when sacrifice fails, chooses the king's daughter as his reward, as is usual in *Märchen*. Compare Melampus and Pero in Greece. The skull in spirit-land here plays a friendly part, in advising the princess, like Proserpine, not to eat among the dead. This caution is found everywhere[xv]—in the Greek version of Orpheus and Eurydice, in the *Kalewala*, and in Scott's "Wandering Willie's Tale," in *Redgauntlet*. Like Orpheus, the girl is not to look back while leaving spirit-land. Her successful escape, by obeying the injunctions of the skull, is unusual.

XXIX. *How the Tortoise overcame the Elephant and the Hippopotamus.*—A "Just So Story," with the tortoise as cunning as Brer Rabbit.

XXX. *Of the Pretty Girl and the Seven Jealous Women.*—Here the good little bird plays the part of the popinjay who "up and spake" with good effect in the first ballads. The useful Ju Ju man divines by casting lots, a common method among the Zulus. The revenge of the pretty girl's father is certainly adequate.

11

XXXI. *How the Cannibals drove the People from Insofan Mountain to the Cross River (Ikom).*—This professes to be historical, and concerns human sacrifices, "to cool the new yams," and cannibalism.

XXXII. is unimportant.

In XXXIII. we find the ordeal poison, which destroys fifty witches.

XXXIV. *The Slave Girl who tried to Kill her Mistress* is a form of our common tale of the waiting-maid who usurps the place of her mistress, the Bride. The resurrection of the Bride from the water, at the cry of her little sister, occurs in a remote quarter, among the Samoyeds in Castren's *Samoyedische Märchen*, but there the opening is in the style of *Asterinos and Pulja (Phrixus and Helle)* in Van Hahn's *Griechische Märchen*. The False Bride story is, in an ancient French *chanson de geste*, part of the legend of[xvi] the mother of Charlemagne. The story also occurs in Callaway's collection of Zulu fairy tales. In the Nigerian version the manners, customs, and cruelties are all thoroughly West African.

XXXV. *The King and the 'Nsiat Bird* accounts, as usual, for the habits of the bird; and also illustrates the widespread custom of killing twins.

XXXVI. reflects the well-known practices of poison and the ordeal by poison.

XXXVII. is another "Just So Story."

XXXVIII. *The Drummer and the Alligators.*—In this grim tale of one of the abominable secret societies the human alligators appear to be regarded as being capable of taking bestial form, like werewolves or the leopards of another African secret society.

XXXIX. and XL. are both picturesque "Just So Stories," so common in the folk-lore of all countries.

The most striking point in the tales is the combination of good humour and good feeling with horrible cruelties, and the reign of terror of the Egbos and lesser societies. European influences can scarcely do much harm, apart from whisky, in Nigeria. As to religion, we do not learn that the Creator receives any sacrifice: in savage and barbaric countries He usually gets none. Only Ju Jus, whether ghosts or fiends in general, are propitiated. The Other is "too high and too far."

I have briefly indicated the stories which have variants in ancient myth and European *Märchen* or fairy tales.

FOOTNOTES

[1]See the Platonic dialogue, Minos, 315-6, and Athamas in Roscher's *Lexikon*.

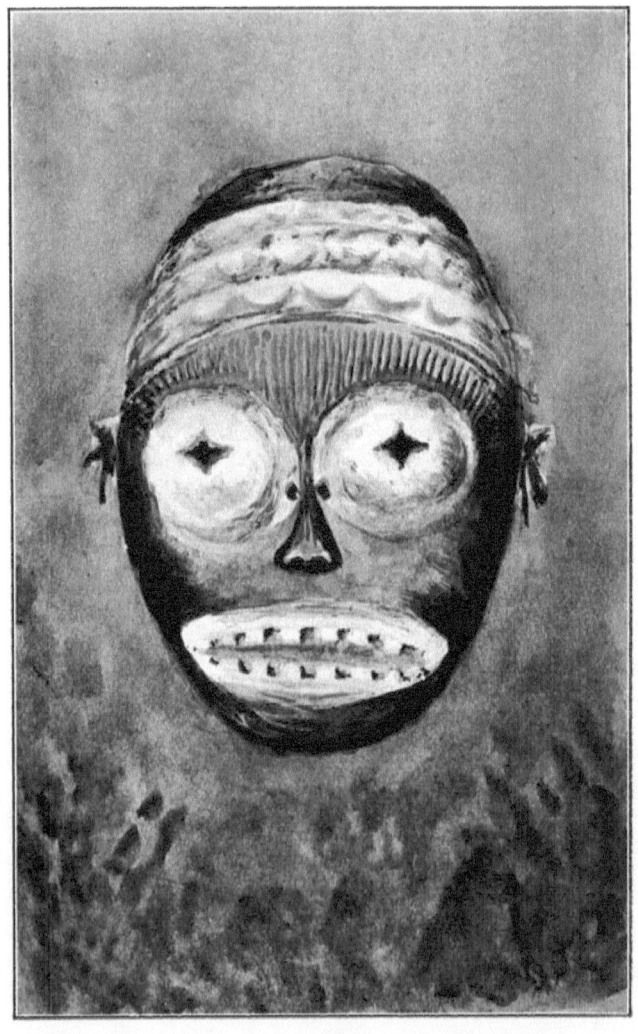

FOLK STORIES
FROM SOUTHERN NIGERIA

[1]

I

The Tortoise with a Pretty Daughter

There was once a king who was very powerful. He had great influence over the wild beasts and animals. Now the tortoise was looked upon as the wisest of all beasts and men. This king had a son named Ekpenyon, to whom he gave fifty young girls as wives, but the prince did not like any of them. The king was very angry at this, and made a law that if any man had a daughter who was finer than the prince's wives, and who found favour in his son's eyes, the girl herself and her father and mother should be killed.

Now about this time the tortoise and his wife had a daughter who was very beautiful. The mother thought it was not safe to keep such a fine child, as the prince might fall in love with her, so she told her husband that her daughter ought to be killed and thrown away into the bush. The tortoise, however, was unwilling, and hid her until she was three years old. One day, when both the tortoise and his wife were away on their farm, the king's[2] son happened to be hunting near their house, and saw a bird perched on the top of the fence round the house. The bird was watching the little girl, and was so entranced with her beauty that he did not notice the prince coming. The prince shot the bird with his bow and arrow, and it dropped inside the fence, so the prince sent his servant to gather it. While the servant was looking for the bird he came across the little girl, and was so struck with her form, that he immediately returned to his master and told him what he had seen. The prince then broke down the fence and found the child, and fell in love with her at once. He stayed and talked with her for a long time, until at last she agreed to become his wife. He then went home, but concealed from his father the fact that he had fallen in love with the beautiful daughter of the tortoise.

But the next morning he sent for the treasurer, and got sixty pieces of cloth[2] and three hundred rods,[3] and sent them to the tortoise. Then in the early afternoon he went down to the tortoise's house, and told him that he wished to marry his daughter. The tortoise saw at once that what he had dreaded had come to pass, and that his life was in danger, so he told the prince that if the king knew, he would kill not only himself (the tortoise), but also his wife and daughter. The prince replied that he would be killed himself before he allowed [3]the tortoise and his wife and daughter to be killed. Eventually, after much argument, the tortoise consented, and agreed to hand his

15

daughter to the prince as his wife when she arrived at the proper age. Then the prince went home and told his mother what he had done. She was in great distress at the thought that she would lose her son, of whom she was very proud, as she knew that when the king heard of his son's disobedience he would kill him. However, the queen, although she knew how angry her husband would be, wanted her son to marry the girl he had fallen in love with, so she went to the tortoise and gave him some money, clothes, yams, and palm-oil as further dowry on her son's behalf in order that the tortoise should not give his daughter to another man. For the next five years the prince was constantly with the tortoise's daughter, whose name was Adet, and when she was about to be put in the fatting house,[4] the prince told his father that he was going to take Adet as his wife. On hearing this the king was very angry, and sent word all round his kingdom that all people should come on a certain day to the market-place to hear the palaver. When the appointed day arrived the market-place was quite full of people, and the stones belonging to the king and queen were placed in the middle of the market-place.

When the king and queen arrived all the people stood up and greeted them, and they then sat down on their stones. The king then told his attendants [4]to bring the girl Adet before him. When she arrived the king was quite astonished at her beauty. He then told the people that he had sent for them to tell them that he was angry with his son for disobeying him and taking Adet as his wife without his knowledge, but that now he had seen her himself he had to acknowledge that she was very beautiful, and that his son had made a good choice. He would therefore forgive his son.

When the people saw the girl they agreed that she was very fine and quite worthy of being the prince's wife, and begged the king to cancel the law he had made altogether, and the king agreed; and as the law had been made under the "Egbo" law, he sent for eight Egbos,[5] and told them that the order was cancelled throughout his kingdom, and that for the future no one would be killed who had a daughter more beautiful than the prince's wives, and gave the Egbos palm wine and money to remove the law, and [5]sent them away. Then he declared that the tortoise's daughter, Adet, should marry his son, and he made them marry the same day. A great feast was then given which lasted for fifty days, and the king killed five cows and gave all the people plenty of foo-foo[6] and palm-oil chop, and placed a large number of pots of palm wine in the streets for the people to drink as they liked. The women brought a big play to the king's compound, and there was singing and dancing kept up day and night during the whole time. The prince and his companions also played in the market square. When the feast was over the king gave half of his kingdom to the tortoise to rule over, and three hundred slaves to work on his farm. The prince also gave his father-in-law two hundred women and one hundred girls to work for him, so the tortoise became one of the richest men in the kingdom. The prince and his wife lived together for a good many years until the king died, when the prince ruled in his place. And all this shows that the tortoise is the wisest of all men and animals.

MORAL.—Always have pretty daughters, as no matter how poor they may be, there is always the chance that the king's son may fall in love with them, and they may thus become members of the royal house and obtain much wealth.

FOOTNOTES

[2]A piece of cloth is generally about 8 yards long by 1 yard broad, and is valued at 5s.

[3]A rod is made of brass, and is worth 3d. It is in the shape of a narrow croquet hoop, about 16 inches long and 6 inches across. A rod is native currency on the Cross River.

[4]The fatting house is a room where a girl is kept for some weeks previous to her marriage. She is given plenty of food, and made as fat as possible, as fatness is looked upon as a great beauty by the Efik people.

[5]The Egbo Society has many branches, extending from Calabar up the Cross River as far as the German Cameroons. Formerly this society used to levy blackmail to a certain extent and collect debts for people. The head Ju Ju, or fetish man, of each society is disguised, and frequently wears a hideous mask. There is a bell tied round his waist, hanging behind and concealed by feathers; this bell makes a noise as he runs. When the Egbo is out no women are allowed outside their houses, and even at the present time the women pretend to be very frightened. The Egbo very often carries a whip in his hand, and hits out blindly at any one he comes across. He runs round the town, followed by young men of his society beating drums and firing off guns. There is generally much drinking going on when the Egbo is playing. There is an Egbo House in most towns, the end part of which is screened off for the Egbo to change in. Inside the house are hung human skulls and the skulls of buffalo, or bush cow, as they are called; also heads of the various antelopes, crocodiles, apes, and other animals which have been killed by the members. The skulls of cows and goats killed by the society are also hung up. A fire is always kept in the Egbo House; and in the morning and late afternoon, the members of the society frequently meet there to drink gin and palm wine.

[6]Foo-foo=yams boiled and mashed up.

[6]

II

How a Hunter obtained Money from his Friends the Leopard, Goat, Bush Cat, and Cock, and how he got out of repaying them

Many years ago there was a Calabar hunter called Effiong, who lived in the bush, killed plenty of animals, and made much money. Everyone in the country knew him, and one of his best friends was a man called Okun, who lived near him. But Effiong was very extravagant, and spent much money in eating and drinking with every one, until at last he became quite poor, so he had to go out hunting again; but now his good luck seemed to have deserted him, for although he worked hard, and hunted day and night, he could not succeed in killing anything. One day, as he was very hungry, he went to his friend Okun and borrowed two hundred rods from him, and told him to come to his house on a certain day to get his money, and he told him to bring his gun, loaded, with him.

Now, some time before this Effiong had made friends with a leopard and a bush cat, whom he had met in the forest whilst on one of his hunting expeditions; and he had also made friends with a goat and a cock at a farm where he had stayed for the night. But though Effiong had borrowed the money from[7] Okun, he could not think how he was to repay it on the day he had promised. At last, however, he thought of a plan, and on the next day he went to his friend the leopard, and asked him to lend him two hundred rods, promising to return the amount to him on the same day as he had promised to pay Okun; and he also told the leopard, that if he were absent when he came for his money, he could kill anything he saw in the house and eat it. The leopard was then to wait until the hunter arrived, when he would pay him the money; and to this the leopard agreed. The hunter then went to his friend the goat, and borrowed two hundred rods from him in the same way. Effiong also went to his friends the bush cat and the cock, and borrowed two hundred rods from each of them on the same conditions, and told each one of them that if he were absent when they arrived, they could kill and eat anything they found about the place.

When the appointed day arrived the hunter spread some corn on the ground, and then went away and left the house deserted. Very early in the morning, soon after he had begun to crow, the cock remembered what the hunter had told him, and walked over to the hunter's house, but found no one there. On looking round, however, he saw some corn on the ground, and, being hungry, he commenced to eat. About this time the bush cat also arrived, and not finding the hunter at home, he, too, looked about, and very soon he espied the cock, who was busy picking up the grains of corn. So the bush cat went up very softly behind and pounced on the cock and killed him at once, and began to eat him. By this time the[8] goat had come for his money; but not finding his friend, he walked about until he came upon the bush cat, who was so intent upon his meal off the cock, that he did not notice the goat approaching; and the goat, being in rather a bad temper at not getting his money, at once charged at the bush cat and knocked him over, butting him with his horns. This the bush cat did not like at all, so, as he was not big enough to fight the goat, he picked up the remains of the cock and ran off with it to the bush, and so lost his money, as he did not await the arrival of the hunter. The goat was thus left master of the situation and started bleating, and this noise attracted the attention of the leopard, who was on his way to receive payment from the hunter. As he got nearer the smell of goat became very strong, and being hungry, for he had not eaten anything for some time, he approached the goat very carefully. Not seeing any one about he stalked the goat and got nearer and nearer, until he was within springing distance. The goat, in the meantime, was grazing quietly, quite unsuspicious of any danger, as he was in his friend the hunter's compound. Now and then he would say Ba!! But most of the time he was busy eating the young grass, and picking up the leaves which had fallen from a tree of which he was very fond. Suddenly the leopard sprang at the goat, and with one crunch at the neck brought him down. The goat was dead almost at once, and the leopard started on his meal.

It was now about eight o'clock in the morning, and Okun, the hunter's friend, having had his early morning meal, went out with his gun to receive payment[9] of the two hundred rods he had lent to the hunter. When he got close to the house he heard a crunching sound, and, being a hunter himself, he approached very cautiously, and looking over the fence saw the leopard only a few yards off busily engaged eating the goat. He took careful aim at the leopard and fired, whereupon the leopard rolled over dead. The death of the leopard meant that four of the hunter's creditors were now disposed of, as the bush cat had killed the cock, the goat had driven the bush cat away (who thus forfeited his claim), and in his turn the goat had been killed by the leopard, who had just been slain by Okun. This meant a saving of eight hundred rods to Effiong; but he was not content with this, and directly he heard the report of the gun he ran out from where he had been hiding all the time, and found the leopard lying dead with Okun standing over it. Then in very strong language Effiong began to upbraid his friend, and asked him why he had killed his old friend the leopard, that nothing would satisfy him but that he should report the whole matter to the king, who would no doubt deal with him as he thought fit. When Effiong said this Okun was frightened, and begged him not to say anything more about the matter, as the king would be angry; but the hunter was obdurate, and refused to listen to him; and at last Okun said, "If you will allow the whole thing to drop and will say no more about it, I will make you a present of the two hundred rods you borrowed from me." This was just what Effiong wanted, but still he did not give in at once; eventually, however, he agreed, and told Okun he might[10] go, and that he would bury the body of his friend the leopard.

Directly Okun had gone, instead of burying the body Effiong dragged it inside the house and skinned it very carefully. The skin he put out to dry in the sun, and covered it with wood ash, and the body he ate. When the skin was well cured the hunter took it to a distant market, where he sold it for much money. And now, whenever a bush cat sees a cock he always kills it, and does so by right, as he takes the cock in part payment of the two hundred rods which the hunter never paid him.

MORAL.—Never lend money to people, because if they cannot pay they will try to kill you or get rid of you in some way, either by poison or by setting bad Ju Ju's for you.

---

[11]

III

The Woman with Two Skins

Eyamba I. of Calabar was a very powerful king. He fought and conquered all the surrounding countries, killing all the old men and women, but the able-bodied men and girls he caught and brought back as slaves, and they worked on the farms until they died.

This king had two hundred wives, but none of them had borne a son to him. His subjects, seeing that he was becoming an old man, begged him to marry one of the spider's daughters, as they always had plenty of children. But when the king saw the spider's daughter he did not like her, as she was ugly, and the people said it was because her mother had had so many children at the same time. However, in order to please his people he married the ugly girl, and placed her among his other wives, but they all complained because she was so ugly, and said she could not live with them. The king, therefore, built her a separate house for herself, where she was given food and drink the same as the other wives. Every one jeered at her on account of her ugliness; but she was not really ugly, but beautiful, as she was born with two skins, and at her birth her mother was made to promise that she should never [12] remove the ugly skin until a certain time arrived save only during the night, and that she must put it on again before dawn. Now the king's head wife knew this, and was very fearful lest the king should find it out and fall in love with the spider's daughter; so she went to a Ju Ju man and offered him two hundred rods to make a potion that would make the king forget altogether that the spider's daughter was his wife. This the Ju Ju man finally consented to do, after much haggling over the price, for three hundred and fifty rods; and he made up some "medicine," which the head wife mixed with the king's food. For some months this had the effect of making the king forget the spider's daughter, and he used to pass quite close to her without recognising her in any way.

20

When four months had elapsed and the king had not once sent for Adiaha (for that was the name of the spider's daughter), she began to get tired, and went back to her parents. Her father, the spider, then took her to another Ju Ju man, who, by making spells and casting lots, very soon discovered that it was the king's head wife who had made the Ju Ju and had enchanted the king so that he would not look at Adiaha. He therefore told the spider that Adiaha should give the king some medicine which he would prepare, which would make the king remember her. He prepared the medicine, for which the spider had to pay a large sum of money; and that very day Adiaha made a small dish of food, into which she had placed the medicine, and presented it to the king. Directly he had eaten the dish his eyes were opened and he recognised his wife, and told her to come to him[13] that very evening. So in the afternoon, being very joyful, she went down to the river and washed, and when she returned she put on her best cloth and went to the king's palace.

Directly it was dark and all the lights were out she pulled off her ugly skin, and the king saw how beautiful she was, and was very pleased with her; but when the cock crowed Adiaha pulled on her ugly skin again, and went back to her own house.

This she did for four nights running, always taking the ugly skin off in the dark, and leaving before daylight in the morning. In course of time, to the great surprise of all the people, and particularly of the king's two hundred wives, she gave birth to a son; but what surprised them most of all was that only one son was born, whereas her mother had always had a great many children at a time, generally about fifty.

The king's head wife became more jealous than ever when Adiaha had a son; so she went again to the Ju Ju man, and by giving him a large present induced him to give her some medicine which would make the king sick and forget his son. And the medicine would then make the king go to the Ju Ju man, who would tell him that it was his son who had made him sick, as he wanted to reign instead of his father. The Ju Ju man would also tell the king that if he wanted to recover he must throw his son away into the water.

And the king, when he had taken the medicine, went to the Ju Ju man, who told him everything as had been arranged with the head wife. But at first the king did not want to destroy his son. Then[14] his chief subjects begged him to throw his son away, and said that perhaps in a year's time he might get another son. So the king at last agreed, and threw his son into the river, at which the mother grieved and cried bitterly.

Then the head wife went again to the Ju Ju man and got more medicine, which made the king forget Adiaha for three years, during which time she was in mourning for her son. She then returned to her father, and he got some more medicine from his Ju Ju man, which Adiaha gave to the king. And the king knew her and called her to him again, and she lived with him as before. Now the Ju Ju who had helped Adiaha's father, the spider, was a Water Ju Ju, and he was ready when the king threw his son into the water, and saved his life and took him home and kept him alive. And the boy grew up very strong.

After a time Adiaha gave birth to a daughter, and her the jealous wife also persuaded the king to throw away. It took a longer time to persuade him, but at last he agreed, and threw his daughter into the water too, and forgot Adiaha again. But the Water Ju Ju was ready again, and when he had saved the little girl, he thought the time had arrived to punish the action of the jealous wife; so he went about amongst the head young men and persuaded them to hold a wrestling match in the market-place every week. This was done, and the Water Ju Ju told the king's son, who had become very strong, and was very like to his father in appearance, that he should go and wrestle, and that no one would be able to stand up before him. It was then arranged that[15] there should be a grand wrestling match, to which all the strongest men in the country were invited, and the king promised to attend with his head wife.

On the day of the match the Water Ju Ju told the king's son that he need not be in the least afraid, and that his Ju Ju was so powerful, that even the strongest and best wrestlers in the country would not be able to stand up against him for even a few minutes. All the people of the country came to see the great contest, to the winner of which the king had promised to present prizes of cloth and money, and all the strongest men came. When they saw the king's son, whom nobody knew, they laughed and said, "Who is this small boy? He can have no chance against us." But when they came to wrestle, they very soon found that they were no match for him. The boy was very strong indeed, beautifully made and good to look upon, and all the people were surprised to see how like he was to the king.

After wrestling for the greater part of the day the king's son was declared the winner, having thrown everyone who had stood up against him; in fact, some of his opponents had been badly hurt, and had their arms or ribs broken owing to the tremendous strength of the boy. After the match was over the king presented him with cloth and money, and invited him to dine with him in the evening. The boy gladly accepted his father's invitation; and after he had had a good wash in the river, put on his cloth and went up to the palace, where he found the head chiefs of the country and some of the king's most favoured wives. They then sat down to their meal, [16] and the king had his own son, whom he did not know, sitting next to him. On the other side of the boy sat the jealous wife, who had been the cause of all the trouble. All through the dinner this woman did her best to make friends with the boy, with whom she had fallen violently in love on account of his beautiful appearance, his strength, and his being the best wrestler in the country. The woman thought to herself, "I will have this boy as

22

my husband, as my husband is now an old man and will surely soon die." The boy, however, who was as wise as he was strong, was quite aware of everything the jealous woman had done, and although he pretended to be very flattered at the advances of the king's head wife, he did not respond very readily, and went home as soon as he could.

When he returned to the Water Ju Ju's house he told him everything that had happened, and the Water Ju Ju said—

"As you are now in high favour with the king, you must go to him to-morrow and beg a favour from him. The favour you will ask is that all the country shall be called together, and that a certain case shall be tried, and that when the case is finished, the man or woman who is found to be in the wrong shall be killed by the Egbos before all the people."

So the following morning the boy went to the king, who readily granted his request, and at once sent all round the country appointing a day for all the people to come in and hear the case tried. Then the boy went back to the Water Ju Ju, who told him to go to his mother and tell her who he was, and that when the day of the trial arrived, she was to[17] take off her ugly skin and appear in all her beauty, for the time had come when she need no longer wear it. This the son did.

When the day of trial arrived, Adiaha sat in a corner of the square, and nobody recognised the beautiful stranger as the spider's daughter. Her son then sat down next to her, and brought his sister with him. Immediately his mother saw her she said—

"This must be my daughter, whom I have long mourned as dead," and embraced her most affectionately.

The king and his head wife then arrived and sat on their stones in the middle of the square, all the people saluting them with the usual greetings. The king then addressed the people, and said that he had called them together to hear a strong palaver at the request of the young man who had been the victor of the wrestling, and who had promised that if the case went against him he would offer up his life to the Egbo. The king also said that if, on the other hand, the case was decided in the boy's favour, then the other party would be killed, even though it were himself or one of his wives; whoever it was would have to take his or her place on the killing-stone and have their heads cut off by the Egbos. To this all the people agreed, and said they would like to hear what the young man had to say. The young man then walked round the square, and bowed to the king and the people, and asked the question, "Am I not worthy to be the son of any chief in the country?" And all the people answered "Yes!"

The boy then brought his sister out into the [18] middle, leading her by the hand. She was a beautiful girl and well made. When everyone had looked at her he said, "Is not my sister worthy to be any chief's daughter?" And the people replied that she was worthy of being any one's daughter, even the king's. Then he called his mother Adiaha, and she came out, looking very beautiful with her best cloth and beads on, and all the people cheered, as they had never seen a finer woman. The boy then asked them, "Is this woman worthy of being the king's wife?" And a shout went up from every one present that she would be a proper wife for the king, and looked as if she would be the mother of plenty of fine healthy sons.

Then the boy pointed out the jealous woman who was sitting next to the king, and told the people his story, how that his mother, who had two skins, was the spider's daughter; how she had married the king, and how the head wife was jealous and had made a bad Ju Ju for the king, which made him forget his wife; how she had persuaded the king to throw himself and his sister into the river, which, as they all knew, had been done, but the Water Ju Ju had saved both of them, and had brought them up.

Then the boy said: "I leave the king and all of you people to judge my case. If I have done wrong, let me be killed on the stone by the Egbos; if, on the other hand, the woman has done evil, then let the Egbos deal with her as you may decide."

When the king knew that the wrestler was his son he was very glad, and told the Egbos to take the jealous woman away, and punish her in accordance with their laws. The Egbos decided that the woman[19] was a witch; so they took her into the forest and tied her up to a stake, and gave her two hundred lashes with a whip made from hippopotamus hide, and then burnt her alive, so that she should not make any more trouble, and her ashes were thrown into the river. The king then embraced his wife and daughter, and told all the people that she, Adiaha, was his proper wife, and would be the queen for the future.

When the palaver was over, Adiaha was dressed in fine clothes and beads, and carried back in state to the palace by the king's servants.

That night the king gave a big feast to all his subjects, and told them how glad he was to get back his beautiful wife whom he had never known properly before, also his son who was stronger than all men, and his fine daughter. The feast continued for a hundred and sixty-six days; and the king made a law that if any woman was found out getting medicine against her husband, she should be killed at once. Then the king built three new compounds, and placed many slaves in them, both men and women. One compound he gave to his wife, another to his son, and the third he gave to his daughter. They all lived together quite happily for some years until the king died, when his son came to the throne and ruled in his stead.

[20]

IV

The King's Magic Drum

Efriam Duke was an ancient king of Calabar. He was a peaceful man, and did not like war. He had a wonderful drum, the property of which, when it was beaten, was always to provide plenty of good food and drink. So whenever any country declared war against him, he used to call all his enemies together and beat his drum; then to the surprise of every one, instead of fighting the people found tables spread with all sorts of dishes, fish, foo-foo, palm-oil chop, soup, cooked yams and ocros, and plenty of palm wine for everybody. In this way he kept all the country quiet, and sent his enemies away with full stomachs, and in a happy and contented frame of mind. There was only one drawback to possessing the drum, and that was, if the owner of the drum walked over any stick on the road or stept over a fallen tree, all the food would immediately go bad, and three hundred Egbo men would appear with sticks and whips and beat the owner of the drum and all the invited guests very severely.

Efriam Duke was a rich man. He had many farms and hundreds of slaves, a large store of kernels on the beach, and many puncheons of palm-oil. He also had fifty wives and many children. The wives[21] were all fine women and healthy; they were also good mothers, and all of them had plenty of children, which was good for the king's house.

Every few months the king used to issue invitations to all his subjects to come to a big feast, even the wild animals were invited; the elephants, hippopotami, leopards, bush cows, and antelopes used to come, for in those days there was no trouble, as they were friendly with man, and when they were at the feast they did not kill one another. All the people and the animals as well were envious of the king's drum and wanted to possess it, but the king would not part with it.

One morning Ikwor Edem, one of the king's wives, took her little daughter down to the spring to wash her, as she was covered with yaws, which are bad sores all over the body. The tortoise happened to be up a palm tree, just over the spring, cutting nuts for his midday meal; and while he was cutting, one of the nuts fell to the ground, just in front of the child. The little girl, seeing the good food, cried for it, and the mother, not knowing any better, picked up the palm nut and gave it to her daughter. Directly the tortoise saw this he climbed down the tree, and asked the woman where his palm nut was. She replied that she had given it to her child to eat. Then the tortoise, who very much wanted the king's drum, thought he would make plenty palaver over this and force the king to give him the drum, so he said to the mother of the child—

"I am a poor man, and I climbed the tree to get food for myself and my family. Then you took my palm nut and gave it to your child. I shall tell the [22] whole matter to the king, and see what he has to say when he hears that one of his wives has stolen my food," for this, as everyone knows, is a very serious crime according to native custom.

Ikwor Edem then said to the tortoise—

"I saw your palm nut lying on the ground, and thinking it had fallen from the tree, I gave it to my little girl to eat, but I did not steal it. My husband the king is a rich man, and if you have any complaint to make against me or my child, I will take you before him."

So when she had finished washing her daughter at the spring she took the tortoise to her husband, and told him what had taken place. The king then asked the tortoise what he would accept as compensation for the loss of his palm nut, and offered him money, cloth, kernels or palm-oil, all of which things the tortoise refused one after the other.

The king then said to the tortoise, "What will you take? You may have anything you like."

And the tortoise immediately pointed to the king's drum, and said that it was the only thing he wanted.

In order to get rid of the tortoise the king said, "Very well, take the drum," but he never told the tortoise about the bad things that would happen to him if he stept over a fallen tree, or walked over a stick on the road.

The tortoise was very glad at this, and carried the drum home in triumph to his wife, and said, "I am now a rich man, and shall do no more work. Whenever I want food, all I have to do is to beat this drum, and food will immediately be brought to me, and plenty to drink."[23]

His wife and children were very pleased when they heard this, and asked the tortoise to get food at once, as they were all hungry. This the tortoise was only too pleased to do, as he wished to show off his newly acquired wealth, and was also rather hungry himself, so he beat the drum in the same way as he had seen the king do when he wanted something to eat, and immediately plenty of food appeared, so they all sat down and made a great feast. The tortoise did this for three days, and everything went well; all his children got fat, and had as much as they could possibly eat. He was therefore very proud of his drum, and in order to display his riches he sent invitations to the king and all the people and animals to come to a feast. When the people received their invitations they laughed, as they knew the tortoise was very poor, so very few attended the feast; but the king, knowing about the drum, came, and when the tortoise beat the drum, the food was brought as usual in great profusion, and all the people sat down and enjoyed their meal very much. They were much astonished that the poor tortoise should be able to entertain so many people, and told all their friends what fine dishes had been placed before them, and that they had never had a better dinner. The people who had not gone were very sorry when they heard this, as a good feast, at somebody else's expense, is not provided every day. After the feast all the people looked upon the tortoise as one of the richest men in the kingdom, and he was very much respected in consequence. No one, except the king, could understand how the poor tortoise could suddenly[24] entertain so lavishly, but they all made up their minds that if the tortoise ever gave another feast, they would not refuse again.

When the tortoise had been in possession of the drum for a few weeks he became lazy and did no work, but went about the country boasting of his riches, and took to drinking too much. One day after he had been drinking a lot of palm wine at a distant farm, he started home carrying his drum; but having had too much to drink, he did not notice a stick in the path. He walked over the stick, and of course the Ju Ju was broken at once. But he did not know this, as nothing happened at the time, and eventually he arrived at his house very tired, and still not very well from having drunk too much. He threw the drum into a corner and went to sleep. When he woke up in the morning the tortoise began to feel hungry, and as his wife and children were calling out for food, he beat the drum; but instead of food being brought, the house was filled with Egbo men, who beat the tortoise, his wife and children, badly. At this the tortoise was very angry, and said to himself—

"I asked every one to a feast, but only a few came, and they had plenty to eat and drink. Now, when I want food for myself and my family, the Egbos come and beat me. Well, I will let the other people share the same fate, as I do not see why I and my family should be beaten when I have given a feast to all people."

He therefore at once sent out invitations to all the men and animals to come to a big dinner the next day at three o'clock in the afternoon.[25]

When the time arrived many people came, as they did not wish to lose the chance of a free meal a second time. Even the sick men, the lame, and the blind got their friends to lead them to the feast. When they had all arrived, with the exception of the king and his wives, who sent excuses, the tortoise beat his drum as usual, and then quickly hid himself under a bench, where he could not be seen. His wife and children he had sent away before the feast, as he knew what would surely happen. Directly he had beaten the drum three hundred Egbo men appeared with whips, and started flogging all the guests, who could not escape, as the doors had been fastened. The beating went on for two hours, and the people were so badly punished, that many of them had to be carried home on the backs of their friends. The leopard was the only one who escaped, as directly he saw the Egbo men arrive he knew that things were likely to be unpleasant, so he gave a big spring and jumped right out of the compound.

When the tortoise was satisfied with the beating the people had received he crept to the door and opened it. The people then ran away, and when the tortoise gave a certain tap on the drum all the Egbo men vanished. The people who had been beaten were so angry, and made so much palaver with the tortoise, that he made up his mind to return the drum to the king the next day. So in the morning the tortoise went to the king and brought the drum with him. He told the king that he was not satisfied with the drum, and wished to exchange it for something else; he did not mind so much what the king gave him so long as he got full value for[26] the drum, and he was quite willing to accept a certain number of slaves, or a few farms, or their equivalent in cloth or rods.

The king, however, refused to do this; but as he was rather sorry for the tortoise, he said he would present him with a magic foo-foo tree, which would provide the tortoise and his family with food, provided he kept a certain condition. This the tortoise gladly consented to do. Now this foo-foo tree only bore fruit once a year, but every day it dropped foo-foo and soup on the ground. And the condition was, that the owner should gather sufficient food for the day, once, and not return again for more. The tortoise, when he had thanked the king for his generosity, went home to his wife and told her to bring her calabashes to the tree. She did so, and they gathered plenty of foo-foo and soup quite sufficient for the whole family for that day, and went back to their house very happy.

That night they all feasted and enjoyed themselves. But one of the sons, who was very greedy, thought to himself—

"I wonder where my father gets all this good food from? I must ask him."

So in the morning he said to his father—

"Tell me where do you get all this foo-foo and soup from?"

But his father refused to tell him, as his wife, who was a cunning woman, said—

"If we let our children know the secret of the foo-foo tree, some day when they are hungry, after we have got our daily supply, one of them may go to the tree and gather more, which will break the Ju Ju."[27]

But the envious son, being determined to get plenty of food for himself, decided to track his father to the place where he obtained the food. This was rather difficult to do, as the tortoise always went out alone, and took the greatest care to prevent any one following him. The boy, however, soon thought of a plan, and got a calabash with a long neck and a hole in the end. He filled the calabash with wood ashes, which he obtained from the fire, and then got a bag which his father always carried on his back when he went out to get food. In the bottom of the bag the boy then made a small hole, and inserted the calabash with the neck downwards, so that when his father walked to the foo-foo tree he would leave a small trail of wood ashes behind him. Then when his father, having slung his bag over his back as usual, set out to get the daily supply of food, his greedy son followed the trail of the wood ashes, taking great care to hide himself and not to let his father perceive that he was being followed. At last the tortoise arrived at the tree, and placed his calabashes on the ground and collected the food for the day, the boy watching him from a distance. When his father had finished and went home the boy also returned, and having had a good meal, said nothing to his parents, but went to bed. The next morning he got some of his brothers, and after his father had finished getting the daily supply, they went to the tree and collected much foo-foo and soup, and so broke the Ju Ju.

At daylight the tortoise went to the tree as usual, but he could not find it, as during the night the whole bush had grown up, and the foo-foo tree was hidden from sight. There was nothing to be seen[28] but a dense mass of prickly tie-tie palm. Then the tortoise at once knew that some one had broken the Ju Ju, and had gathered foo-foo from the tree twice in the same day; so he returned very sadly to his house, and told his wife. He then called all his family together and told them what had happened, and asked them who had done this evil thing. They all denied having had anything to do with the tree, so the tortoise in despair brought all his family to the place where the foo-foo tree had been, but which was now all prickly tie-tie palm, and said—

"My dear wife and children, I have done all that I can for you, but you have broken my Ju Ju; you must therefore for the future live on the tie-tie palm."

So they made their home underneath the prickly tree, and from that day you will always find tortoises living under the prickly tie-tie palm, as they have nowhere else to go to for food.

---

[29]

V

Ituen and the King's Wife

Ituen was a young man of Calabar. He was the only child of his parents, and they were extremely fond of him, as he was of fine proportions and very good to look upon. They were poor people, and when Ituen grew up and became a man, he had very little money indeed, in fact he had so little food, that every day it was his custom to go to the market carrying an empty bag, into which he used to put anything eatable he could find after the market was over.

At this time Offiong was king. He was an old man, but he had plenty of wives. One of these women, named Attem, was quite young and very good-looking. She did not like her old husband, but wished for a young and handsome husband. She therefore told her servant to go round the town and the market to try and find such a man and to bring him at night by the side door to her house, and she herself would let him in, and would take care that her husband did not discover him.

That day the servant went all round the town, but failed to find any young man good-looking enough. She was just returning to report her ill-success when, on passing through the market-place, she saw Ituen[30] picking up the remains of corn and other things which had been left on the ground. She was immediately struck with his fine appearance and strength, and saw that he was just the man to make a proper lover for her mistress, so she went up to him, and said that the queen had sent for him, as she was so taken with his good looks. At first Ituen was frightened and refused to go, as he knew that if the King discovered him he would be killed. However, after much persuasion he consented, and agreed to go to the queen's side door when it was dark.

When night came he went with great fear and trembling, and knocked very softly at the queen's door. The door was opened at once by the queen herself, who was dressed in all her best clothes, and had many necklaces, beads, and anklets on. Directly she saw Ituen she fell in love with him at once, and praised his good looks and his shapely limbs. She then told her servant to bring water and clothes, and after he had had a good wash and put on a clean cloth, he rejoined the queen. She hid him in her house all the night.

In the morning when he wished to go she would not let him, but, although it was very dangerous, she hid him in the house, and secretly conveyed food and clothes to him. Ituen stayed there for two weeks, and then he said that it was time for him to go and see his mother, but the queen persuaded him to stay another week, much against his will.

When the time came for him to depart, the queen got together fifty carriers with presents for Ituen's mother who, she knew, was a poor woman. Ten [31] slaves carried three hundred rods; the other forty carried yams, pepper, salt, tobacco, and cloth. When all the presents arrived Ituen's mother was very pleased and embraced her son, and noticed with pleasure that he was looking well, and was dressed in much finer clothes than usual; but when she heard that he had attracted the queen's attention she was frightened, as she knew the penalty imposed on any one who attracted the attention of one of the king's wives.

Ituen stayed for a month in his parents' house and worked on the farm; but the queen could not be without her lover any longer, so she sent for him to go to her at once. Ituen went again, and, as before, arrived at night, when the queen was delighted to see him again.

In the middle of the night some of the king's servants, who had been told the story by the slaves who had carried the presents to Ituen's mother, came into the queen's room and surprised her there with Ituen. They hastened to the king, and told him what they had seen. Ituen was then made a prisoner, and the king sent out to all his people to attend at the palaver house to hear the case tried. He also ordered eight Egbos to attend armed with machetes. When the case was tried Ituen was found guilty, and the king told the eight Egbo men to take him into the bush and deal with him according to native custom. The Egbos then took Ituen into the bush and tied him up to a tree; then with a sharp knife they cut off his lower jaw, and carried it to the king.

When the queen heard the fate of her lover she was very sad, and cried for three days. This made[32] the king angry, so he told the Egbos to deal with his wife and her servant according to their law. They took the queen and the servant into the bush, where Ituen was still tied up to the tree dying and in great pain. Then, as the queen had nothing to say in her defence, they tied her and the girl up to different trees, and cut the queen's lower jaw off in the same way as they had her lover's. The Egbos then put out both the eyes of the servant, and left all three to die of starvation. The king then made an Egbo law that for the future no one belonging to Ituen's family was to go into the market on market day, and that no one was to pick up the rubbish in the market. The king made an exception to the law in favour of the vulture and the dog, who were not considered very fine people, and would not be likely to run off with one of the king's wives, and that is why you still find vultures and dogs doing scavenger in the market-places even at the present time.

[33]

VI

AFRICAN SCHOLAR PUBLICATIONS
www.lulu.com/egipt

Of the Pretty Stranger who Killed the King

Mbotu was a very famous king of Old Town, Calabar. He was frequently at war, and was always successful, as he was a most skilful leader. All the prisoners he took were made slaves. He therefore became very rich, but, on the other hand, he had many enemies. The people of Itu in particular were very angry with him and wanted to kill him, but they were not strong enough to beat Mbotu in a pitched battle, so they had to resort to craft. The Itu people had an old woman who was a witch and could turn herself into whatever she pleased, and when she offered to kill Mbotu, the people were very glad, and promised her plenty of money and cloth if she succeeded in ridding them of their worst enemy. The witch then turned herself into a young and pretty girl, and having armed herself with a very sharp knife, which she concealed in her bosom, she went to Old Town, Calabar, to seek the king.

It happened that when she arrived there was a big play being held in the town, and all the people from the surrounding country had come in to dance and feast. Oyaikan, the witch, went to the play, and walked about so that everyone could see her. Directly she appeared the people all marvelled at[34] her beauty, and said that she was as beautiful as the setting sun when all the sky was red. Word was quickly brought to king Mbotu, who, it was well known, was fond of pretty girls, and he sent for her at once, all the people agreeing that she was quite worthy of being the king's wife. When she appeared before him he fancied her so much, that he told her he would marry her that very day. Oyaikan was very pleased at this, as she had never expected to get her opportunity so quickly. She therefore prepared a dainty meal for the king, into which she placed a strong medicine to make the king sleep, and then went down to the river to wash.

When she had finished it was getting dark, so she went to the king's compound, carrying her dish on her head, and was at once shown in to the king, who embraced her affectionately. She then offered him the food, which she said, quite truly, she had prepared with her own hands. The king ate the whole dish, and immediately began to feel very sleepy, as the medicine was strong and took effect quickly.

They retired to the king's chamber, and the king went to sleep at once. About midnight, when all the town was quiet, Oyaikan drew her knife from her bosom and cut the king's head off. She put the head in a bag and went out very softly, shutting and barring the door behind her. Then she walked through the town without any one observing her, and went straight to Itu, where she placed king Mbotu's head before her own king.

When the people heard that the witch had been successful and that their enemy was dead, there was great rejoicing, and the king of Itu at once made up[35] his mind to attack Old Town, Calabar. He therefore got his fighting men together and took them in canoes by the creeks to Old Town, taking care that no one carried word to Calabar that he was coming.

The morning following the murder of Mbotu his people were rather surprised that he did not appear at his usual time, so his head wife knocked at his door. Not receiving any answer she called the household together, and they broke open the door. When they entered the room they found the king lying dead on his bed covered in blood, but his head was missing. At this a great shout went up, and the whole town mourned. Although they missed the pretty stranger, they never connected her in their minds with the death of their king, and were quite unsuspicious of any danger, and were unprepared for fighting. In the middle of the mourning, while they were all dancing, crying, and drinking palm wine, the king of Itu with all his soldiers attacked Old Town, taking them quite by surprise, and as their leader was dead, the Calabar people were very soon defeated, and many killed and taken prisoners.

MORAL.—Never marry a stranger, no matter how pretty she may be.

---

[36]

VII

Why the Bat flies by Night

A bush rat called Oyot was a great friend of Emiong, the bat; they always fed together, but the bat was jealous of the bush rat. When the bat cooked the food it was always very good, and the bush rat said, "How is it that when you make the soup it is so tasty?"

The bat replied, "I always boil myself in the water, and my flesh is so sweet, that the soup is good."

He then told the bush rat that he would show him how it was done; so he got a pot of warm water, which he told the bush rat was boiling water, and jumped into it, and very shortly afterwards came out again. When the soup was brought it was as strong and good as usual, as the bat had prepared it beforehand.

The bush rat then went home and told his wife that he was going to make good soup like the bat's. He therefore told her to boil some water, which she did. Then, when his wife was not looking, he jumped into the pot, and was very soon dead.

When his wife looked into the pot and saw the dead body of her husband boiling she was very angry, and reported the matter to the king, who[37] gave orders that the bat should be made a prisoner. Every one turned out to catch the bat, but as he expected trouble he flew away into the bush and hid himself. All day long the people tried to catch him, so he had to change his habits, and only came out to feed when it was dark, and that is why you never see a bat in the daytime.

---

[38]

VIII

The Disobedient Daughter who Married a Skull

Effiong Edem was a native of Cobham Town. He had a very fine daughter, whose name was Afiong. All the young men in the country wanted to marry her on account of her beauty; but she refused all offers of marriage in spite of repeated entreaties from her parents, as she was very vain, and said she would only marry the best-looking man in the country, who would have to be young and strong, and capable of loving her properly. Most of the men her parents wanted her to marry, although they were rich, were old men and ugly, so the girl continued to disobey her parents, at which they were very much grieved. The skull who lived in the spirit land heard of the beauty of this Calabar virgin, and thought he would like to possess her; so he went about amongst his friends and borrowed different parts of the body from them, all of the best. From one he got a good head, another lent him a body, a third gave him strong arms, and a fourth lent him a fine pair of legs. At last he was complete, and was a very perfect specimen of manhood.

He then left the spirit land and went to Cobham market, where he saw Afiong, and admired her very much.[39]

About this time Afiong heard that a very fine man had been seen in the market, who was better-looking than any of the natives. She therefore went to the market at once, and directly she saw the Skull in his borrowed beauty, she fell in love with him, and invited him to her house. The Skull was delighted, and went home with her, and on his arrival was introduced by the girl to her parents, and immediately asked their consent to marry their daughter. At first they refused, as they did not wish her to marry a stranger, but at last they agreed.

He lived with Afiong for two days in her parents' house, and then said he wished to take his wife back to his country, which was far off. To this the girl readily agreed, as he was such a fine man, but her parents tried to persuade her not to go. However, being very headstrong, she made up her mind to go, and they started off together. After they had been gone a few days the father consulted his Ju Ju man, who by casting lots very soon discovered that his daughter's husband belonged to the spirit land, and that she would surely be killed. They therefore all mourned her as dead.

After walking for several days, Afiong and the Skull crossed the border between the spirit land and the human country. Directly they set foot in the spirit land, first of all one man came to the Skull and demanded his legs, then another his head, and the next his body, and so on, until in a few minutes the skull was left by itself in all its natural ugliness. At this the girl was very frightened, and wanted to return home, but the skull would not allow this, and ordered her to go with him. When they arrived at[40] the skull's house they found his mother, who was a very old woman quite incapable of doing any work, who could only creep about. Afiong tried her best to help her, and cooked her food, and brought water and firewood for the old woman. The old creature was very grateful for these attentions, and soon became quite fond of Afiong.

One day the old woman told Afiong that she was very sorry for her, but all the people in the spirit land were cannibals, and when they heard there was a human being in their country, they would come down and kill her and eat her. The skull's mother then hid Afiong, and as she had looked after her so well, she promised she would send her back to her country as soon as possible, providing that she promised for the future to obey her parents. This Afiong readily consented to do. Then the old woman sent for the spider, who was a very clever hairdresser, and made him dress Afiong's hair in the latest fashion. She also presented her with anklets and other things on account of her kindness. She then made a Ju Ju and called the winds to come and convey Afiong to her home. At first a violent tornado came, with thunder, lightning and rain, but the skull's mother sent him away as unsuitable. The next wind to come was a gentle breeze, so she told the breeze to carry Afiong to her mother's house, and said good-bye to her. Very soon afterwards the breeze deposited Afiong outside her home, and left her there.

When the parents saw their daughter they were very glad, as they had for some months given her up as lost. The father spread soft animals' skins[41] on the ground from where his daughter was standing all the way to the house, so that her feet should not be soiled. Afiong then walked to the house, and her father called all the young girls who belonged to Afiong's company to come and dance, and the feasting and dancing was kept up for eight days and nights. When the rejoicing was over, the father reported what had happened to the head chief of the town. The chief then passed a law that parents should never allow their daughters to marry strangers who came from a far country. Then the father told his daughter to marry a friend of his, and she willingly consented, and lived with him for many years, and had many children.

[42]

IX

The King who Married the Cock's Daughter

King Effiom of Duke Town, Calabar, was very fond of pretty maidens, and whenever he heard of a girl who was unusually good-looking, he always sent for her, and if she took his fancy, he made her one of his wives. This he could afford to do, as he was a rich man, and could pay any dowry which the parents asked, most of his money having been made by buying and selling slaves.

Effiom had two hundred and fifty wives, but he was never content, and wanted to have all the finest women in the land. Some of the king's friends, who were always on the look-out for pretty girls, told Effiom that the Cock's daughter was a lovely virgin, and far superior to any of the king's wives. Directly the king heard this he sent for the Cock, and said he intended to have his daughter as one of his wives. The Cock, being a poor man, could not resist the order of the king, so he brought his daughter, who was very good-looking and pleased the king immensely. When the king had paid the Cock a dowry of six puncheons of palm-oil, the Cock told Effiom that if he married his daughter he must not forget that she had the natural instincts of a hen,[43] and that he should not blame Adia unen (his daughter) if she picked up corn whenever she saw it. The king replied that he did not mind what she ate so long as he possessed her.

The king then took Adia unen as his wife, and liked her so much, that he neglected all his other wives, and lived entirely with Adia unen, as she suited him exactly and pleased him more than any of his other wives. She also amused the king, and played with him and enticed him in so many different ways that he could not live without her, and always had her with him to the exclusion of his former favourites, whom he would not even speak to or notice in any way when he met them. This so enraged the neglected wives that they met together, and although they all hated one another, they agreed so far that they hated the Cock's daughter more than any one, as now that she had come to the king none of them ever had a chance with him. Formerly the king, although he always had his favourites, used to favour different girls with his attentions when they pleased him particularly. That was very different in their opinion to being excluded from his presence and all his affections being concentrated on one girl, who received all his love and embraces. In consequence of this they were very angry, and determined if possible to disgrace Adia unen. After much discussion, one of the wives, who was the last favourite, and whom the arrival of the Cock's daughter had displaced, said: "This girl, whom we all hate, is, after all, only a Cock's daughter, and we can easily disgrace her in the king's eyes, as I heard her father [44] tell the king that she could not resist corn, no matter how it was thrown about."

Very shortly after the king's wives had determined to try and disgrace Adia unen, all the people of the country came to pay homage to the king. This was done three times a year, the people bringing yams, fowls, goats, and new corn as presents, and the king entertained them with a feast of foo-foo, palm-oil chop, and tombo.[7] A big dance was also held, which was usually kept up for several days and nights. Early in the morning the king's head wife told her servant to wash one head of corn, and when all the people were present she was to bring it in a calabash and throw it on the ground and then walk away. The corn was to be thrown in front of Adia unen, so that all the people and chiefs could see.

About ten o'clock, when all the chiefs and people had assembled, and the king had taken his seat on his big wooden chair, the servant girl came and threw the corn on the ground as she had been ordered. Directly she had done this Adia unen started towards the corn, picked it up, and began to eat. At this all the people laughed, and the king was very angry and ashamed. The king's wives and many people said that they thought the king's finest wife would have learnt better manners than to pick up corn which had been thrown away as refuse. Others said: "What can you expect from a Cock's daughter? She should not be blamed for obeying [45]her natural instincts." But the king was so vexed, that he told one of his servants to pack up Adia unen's things and take them to her father's house. And this was done, and Aida unen returned to her parents.

That night the king's third wife, who was a friend of Adia unen's, talked the whole matter over with the king, and explained to him that it was entirely owing to the jealousy of his head wife that Adia unen had been disgraced. She also told him that the whole thing had been arranged beforehand in order that the king should get rid of Adia unen, of whom all the other wives were jealous. When the king heard this he was very angry, and made up his mind to send the jealous woman back to her parents empty-handed, without her clothes and presents. When she arrived at her father's house the parents refused to take her in, as she had been given as a wife to the king, and whenever the parents wanted anything, they could always get it at the palace. It was therefore a great loss to them. She was thus turned into the streets, and walked about very miserable, and after a time died, very poor and starving.

The king grieved so much at having been compelled to send his favourite wife Adia unen away, that he died the following year. And when the people saw that their king had died of a broken heart, they passed a law that for the future no one should marry any bird or animal.

FOOTNOTES

[7]Tombo is an intoxicating drink made from the juice which is extracted from the tombo palm, and which ferments very quickly. It is drawn from the tree twice a day—in the morning very early, and again in the afternoon.

---

[46]

X

The Woman, the Ape, and the Child

Okun Archibong was one of King Archibong's slaves, and lived on a farm near Calabar. He was a hunter, and used to kill bush buck and other kinds of antelopes and many monkeys. The skins he used to dry in the sun, and when they were properly cured, he used to sell them in the market; the monkey skins were used for making drums, and the antelope skins were used for sitting mats. The flesh, after it had been well smoked over a wood fire, he also sold, but he did not make much money.

Okun Archibong married a slave woman of Duke's house named Nkoyo. He paid a small dowry to the Dukes, took his wife home to his farm, and in the dry season time she had a son. About four months after the birth of the child Nkoyo took him to the farm while her husband was absent hunting. She placed the little boy under a shady tree and went about her work, which was clearing the ground for the yams which would be planted about two months before the rains. Every day while the mother was working a big ape used to come from the forest and play with the little boy; he used to hold him in his arms and carry him up a tree, and when Nkoyo had finished her work, he used to bring the baby back to her. There was a hunter named Edem Effiong who[47] had for a long time been in love with Nkoyo, and had made advances to her, but she would have nothing to do with him, as she was very fond of her husband. When she had her little child Effiong Edem was very jealous, and meeting her one day on the farm without her baby, he said: "Where is your baby?" And she replied that a big ape had taken it up a tree and was looking after it for her. When Effiong Edem saw that the ape was a big one, he made up his mind to tell Nkoyo's husband. The very next day he told Okun Archibong that he had seen his wife in the forest with a big ape. At first Okun would not believe this, but the hunter told him to come with him and he could see it with his own eyes. Okun Archibong therefore made up his mind to kill the ape. The next day he went with the other hunter to the farm and saw the ape up a tree playing with his son, so he took very careful aim and shot the ape, but it was not quite killed. It was so angry, and its strength was so great, that it tore the child limb from limb and threw it to the ground. This so enraged Okun Archibong that seeing his wife standing near he shot her also. He then ran home and told King Archibong what had taken place. This king was very brave and fond of fighting, so as he knew that King Duke would be certain to make war upon him, he immediately called in all his fighting men. When he was quite prepared he sent a messenger to tell King Duke what had happened. Duke was very angry, and sent the messenger back to King Archibong to say that he must send the hunter to him, so that he could kill him in any way he pleased. This Archibong refused to do, and said[48] he would rather fight. Duke then got his men together, and both sides met and fought in the market square. Thirty men were killed of Duke's men, and twenty were killed on Archibong's side; there were also many wounded. On the whole King Archibong had the best of the fighting, and drove King Duke back. When the fighting was at its hottest the other chiefs sent out all the Egbo men with drums and stopped the fight, and the next day the palaver was tried in Egbo house. King Archibong was found guilty, and was ordered to pay six thousand rods to King Duke. He refused to pay this amount to Duke, and said he would rather go on fighting, but he did not mind paying the six thousand rods to the town, as the Egbos had decided the case. They were about to commence fighting again when the whole country rose up and said they would not have any more fighting, as Archibong said to Duke that the woman's death was not really the fault of his slave Okun Archibong, but of Effiong Edem, who made the false report. When Duke heard this he agreed to leave the whole matter to the chiefs to decide, and Effiong Edem was called to take his place on the stone. He was tried and found guilty, and two Egbos came out armed with cutting whips and gave him two hundred lashes on his bare back, and then cut off his head and sent it to Duke, who placed it before his Ju Ju. From that time to the present all apes and monkeys have been frightened of human beings; and even of little children. The Egbos also passed a law that a chief should not allow one of his men slaves to marry a woman slave of another house, as it would probably lead to fighting.

[49]

XI

The Fish and the Leopard's Wife; or, Why the Fish lives in the Water

Many years ago, when King Eyo was ruler of Calabar, the fish used to live on the land; he was a great friend of the leopard, and frequently used to go to his house in the bush, where the leopard entertained him. Now the leopard had a very fine wife, with whom the fish fell in love. And after a time, whenever the leopard was absent in the bush, the fish used to go to his house and make love to the leopard's wife, until at last an old woman who lived near informed the leopard what happened whenever he went away. At first the leopard would not believe that the fish, who had been his friend for so long, would play such a low trick, but one night he came back unexpectedly, and found the fish and his wife together; at this the leopard was very angry, and was going to kill the fish, but he thought as the fish had been his friend for so long, he would not deal with him himself, but would report his behaviour to King Eyo. This he did, and the king held a big palaver, at which the leopard stated his case quite shortly, but when the fish was put upon his defence he had nothing to say, so the king addressing his subjects said, "This [50] is a very bad case, as the fish has been the leopard's friend, and has been trusted by him, but the fish has taken advantage of his friend's absence, and has betrayed him." The king, therefore, made an order that for the future the fish should live in the water, and that if he ever came on the land he should die; he also said that all men and animals should kill and eat the fish whenever they could catch him, as a punishment for his behaviour with his friend's wife.

[51]

XII

AFRICAN SCHOLAR PUBLICATIONS
www.lulu.com/egipt

Why the Bat is Ashamed to be seen in the Daytime

There was once an old mother sheep who had seven lambs, and one day the bat, who was about to make a visit to his father-in-law who lived a long day's march away, went to the old sheep and asked her to lend him one of her young lambs to carry his load for him. At first the mother sheep refused, but as the young lamb was anxious to travel and see something of the world, and begged to be allowed to go, at last she reluctantly consented. So in the morning at daylight the bat and the lamb set off together, the lamb carrying the bat's drinking-horn. When they reached half-way, the bat told the lamb to leave the horn underneath a bamboo tree. Directly he arrived at the house, he sent the lamb back to get the horn. When the lamb had gone the bat's father-in-law brought him food, and the bat ate it all, leaving nothing for the lamb. When the lamb returned, the bat said to him, "Hullo! you have arrived at last I see, but you are too late for food; it is all finished." He then sent the lamb back to the tree with the horn, and when the lamb returned again it was late, and he went supperless to bed. The next day, just before it was time for[52] food, the bat sent the lamb off again for the drinking-horn, and when the food arrived the bat, who was very greedy, ate it all up a second time. This mean behaviour on the part of the bat went on for four days, until at last the lamb became quite thin and weak. The bat decided to return home the next day, and it was all the lamb could do to carry his load. When he got home to his mother the lamb complained bitterly of the treatment he had received from the bat, and was baa-ing all night, complaining of pains in his inside. The old mother sheep, who was very fond of her children, determined to be revenged on the bat for the cruel way he had starved her lamb; she therefore decided to consult the tortoise, who, although very poor, was considered by all people to be the wisest of all animals. When the old sheep had told the whole story to the tortoise, he considered for some time, and then told the sheep that she might leave the matter entirely to him, and he would take ample revenge on the bat for his cruel treatment of her son.

Very soon after this the bat thought he would again go and see his father-in-law, so he went to the mother sheep again and asked her for one of her sons to carry his load as before. The tortoise, who happened to be present, told the bat that he was going in that direction, and would cheerfully carry his load for him. They set out on their journey the following day, and when they arrived at the half-way halting-place the bat pursued the same tactics that he had on the previous occasion. He told the tortoise to hide his drinking-horn under the same tree as the lamb had hidden it before; this the tortoise did,[53] but when the bat was not looking he picked up the drinking-horn again and hid it in his bag. When they arrived at the house the tortoise hung the horn up out of sight in the back yard, and then sat down in the house. Just before it was time for food the bat sent the tortoise to get the drinking-horn, and the tortoise went outside into the yard, and waited until he heard that the beating of the boiled yams into foo-foo had

41

finished; he then went into the house and gave the drinking-horn to the bat, who was so surprised and angry, that when the food was passed he refused to eat any of it, so the tortoise ate it all; this went on for four days, until at last the bat became as thin as the poor little lamb had been on the previous occasion. At last the bat could stand the pains of his inside no longer, and secretly told his mother-in-law to bring him food when the tortoise was not looking. He said, "I am now going to sleep for a little, but you can wake me up when the food is ready." The tortoise, who had been listening all the time, being hidden in a corner out of sight, waited until the bat was fast asleep, and then carried him very gently into the next room and placed him on his own bed; he then very softly and quietly took off the bat's cloth and covered himself in it, and lay down where the bat had been; very soon the bat's mother-in-law brought the food and placed it next to where the bat was supposed to be sleeping, and having pulled his cloth to wake him, went away. The tortoise then got up and ate all the food; when he had finished he carried the bat back again, and took some of the palm-oil and foo-foo and placed it inside the bat's lips while[54] he was asleep; then the tortoise went to sleep himself. In the morning when he woke up the bat was more hungry than ever, and in a very bad temper, so he sought out his mother-in-law and started scolding her, and asked her why she had not brought his food as he had told her to do. She replied she had brought his food, and that he had eaten it; but this the bat denied, and accused the tortoise of having eaten the food. The woman then said she would call the people in and they should decide the matter; but the tortoise slipped out first and told the people that the best way to find out who had eaten the food was to make both the bat and himself rinse their mouths out with clean water into a basin. This they decided to do, so the tortoise got his tooth-stick which he always used, and having cleaned his teeth properly, washed his mouth out, and returned to the house.

When all the people had arrived the woman told them how the bat had abused her, and as he still maintained stoutly that he had had no food for five days, the people said that both he and the tortoise should wash their mouths out with clean water into two clean calabashes; this was done, and at once it could clearly be seen that the bat had been eating, as there were distinct traces of the palm-oil and foo-foo which the tortoise had put inside his lips floating on the water. When the people saw this they decided against the bat, and he was so ashamed that he ran away then and there, and has ever since always hidden himself in the bush during the daytime, so that no one could see him, and only comes out at night to get his food.[55]

The next day the tortoise returned to the mother sheep and told her what he had done, and that the bat was for ever disgraced. The old sheep praised him very much, and told all her friends, in consequence of which the reputation of the tortoise for wisdom was greatly increased throughout the whole country.

[56]

XIII

Why the Worms live Underneath the Ground

When Eyo III. was ruling over all men and animals, he had a very big palaver house to which he used to invite his subjects at intervals to feast. After the feast had been held and plenty of tombo had been drunk, it was the custom of the people to make speeches. One day after the feast the head driver ant got up and said he and his people were stronger than any one, and that no one, not even the elephant, could stand before him, which was quite true. He was particularly offensive in his allusions to the worms (whom he disliked very much), and said they were poor wriggling things.

The worms were very angry and complained, so the king said that the best way to decide the question who was the stronger was for both sides to meet on the road and fight the matter out between themselves to a finish. He appointed the third day from the feast for the contest, and all the people turned out to witness the battle.

The driver ants left their nest in the early morning in thousands and millions, and, as is their custom, marched in a line about one inch broad densely packed, so that it was like a dark-brown band moving over the country. In front of the advancing column[57] they had out their scouts, advance guard, and flankers, and the main body followed in their millions close behind.

When they came to the battlefield the moving band spread out, and as the thousands upon thousands of ants rolled up, the whole piece of ground was a moving mass of ants and bunches of struggling worms. The fight was over in a very few minutes, as the worms were bitten in pieces by the sharp pincer-like mouths of the driver ants. The few worms who survived squirmed away and buried themselves out of sight.

King Eyo decided that the driver ants were easy winners, and ever since the worms have always been afraid and have lived underground; and if they happen to come to the surface after the rain they hide themselves under the ground whenever anything approaches, as they fear all people.

[58]

XIV

The Elephant and the Tortoise; or, Why the Worms are Blind and Why the Elephant has Small Eyes

When Ambo was king of Calabar, the elephant was not only a very big animal, but he had eyes in proportion to his immense bulk. In those days men and animals were friends, and all mixed together quite freely. At regular intervals King Ambo used to give a feast, and the elephant used to eat more than any one, although the hippopotamus used to do his best; however, not being as big as the elephant, although he was very fat, he was left a long way behind.

As the elephant ate so much at these feasts, the tortoise, who was small but very cunning, made up his mind to put a stop to the elephant eating more than a fair share of the food provided. He therefore placed some dry kernels and shrimps, of which the elephant was very fond, in his bag, and went to the elephant's house to make an afternoon call.

When the tortoise arrived the elephant told him to sit down, so he made himself comfortable, and, having shut one eye, took one palm kernel and a shrimp out of his bag, and commenced to eat them with much relish.[59]

When the elephant saw the tortoise eating, he said, as he was always hungry himself, "You seem to have some good food there; what are you eating?"

The tortoise replied that the food was "sweet too much," but was rather painful to him, as he was eating one of his own eyeballs; and he lifted up his head, showing one eye closed.

The elephant then said, "If the food is so good, take out one of my eyes and give me the same food."

The tortoise, who was waiting for this, knowing how greedy the elephant was, had brought a sharp knife with him for that very purpose, and said to the elephant, "I cannot reach your eye, as you are so big."

The elephant then took the tortoise up in his trunk and lifted him up. As soon as he came near the elephant's eye, with one quick scoop of the sharp knife he had the elephant's right eye out. The elephant trumpeted with pain; but the tortoise gave him some of the dried kernels and shrimps, and they so pleased the elephant's palate that he soon forgot the pain.

44

Very soon the elephant said, "That food is so sweet, I must have some more"; but the tortoise told him that before he could have any the other eye must come out. To this the elephant agreed; so the tortoise quickly got his knife to work, and very soon the elephant's left eye was on the ground, thus leaving the elephant quite blind. The tortoise then slid down the elephant's trunk on to the ground and hid himself. The elephant then began to make a great noise, and started pulling trees down and doing much damage, calling out for the tortoise;[60] but of course he never answered, and the elephant could not find him.

The next morning, when the elephant heard the people passing, he asked them what the time was, and the bush buck, who was nearest, shouted out, "The sun is now up, and I am going to market to get some yams and fresh leaves for my food."

Then the elephant perceived that the tortoise had deceived him, and began to ask all the passers-by to lend him a pair of eyes, as he could not see, but every one refused, as they wanted their eyes themselves. At last the worm grovelled past, and seeing the big elephant, greeted him in his humble way. He was much surprised when the king of the forest returned his salutation, and very much flattered also.

The elephant said, "Look here, worm, I have mislaid my eyes. Will you lend me yours for a few days? I will return them next market-day."

The worm was so flattered at being noticed by the elephant that he gladly consented, and took his eyes out—which, as everyone knows, were very small—and gave them to the elephant. When the elephant had put the worm's eyes into his own large eye-sockets, the flesh immediately closed round them so tightly that when the market-day arrived it was impossible for the elephant to get them out again to return to the worm; and although the worm repeatedly made applications to the elephant to return his eyes, the elephant always pretended not to hear, and sometimes used to say in a very loud voice, "If there are any worms about, they had better get out of my way, as they are so small I cannot see them,[61] and if I tread on them they will be squashed into a nasty mess."

Ever since then the worms have been blind, and for the same reason elephants have such small eyes, quite out of proportion to the size of their huge bodies.

[62]

XV

Why a Hawk kills Chickens

In the olden days there was a very fine young hen who lived with her parents in the bush.

One day a hawk was hovering round, about eleven o'clock in the morning, as was his custom, making large circles in the air and scarcely moving his wings. His keen eyes were wide open, taking in everything (for nothing moving ever escapes the eyes of a hawk, no matter how small it may be or how high up in the air the hawk may be circling). This hawk saw the pretty hen picking up some corn near her father's house. He therefore closed his wings slightly, and in a second of time was close to the ground; then spreading his wings out to check his flight, he alighted close to the hen and perched himself on the fence, as a hawk does not like to walk on the ground if he can help it.

He then greeted the young hen with his most enticing whistle, and offered to marry her. She agreed, so the hawk spoke to the parents, and paid the agreed amount of dowry, which consisted mostly of corn, and the next day took the young hen off to his home.

Shortly after this a young cock who lived near the hen's former home found out where she was living,[63] and having been in love with her for some months—in fact, ever since his spurs had grown—determined to try and make her return to her own country. He therefore went at dawn, and, having flapped his wings once or twice, crowed in his best voice to the young hen. When she heard the sweet voice of the cock she could not resist his invitation, so she went out to him, and they walked off together to her parent's house, the young cock strutting in front crowing at intervals.

The hawk, who was hovering high up in the sky, quite out of sight of any ordinary eye, saw what had happened, and was very angry. He made up his mind at once that he would obtain justice from the king, and flew off to Calabar, where he told the whole story, and asked for immediate redress. So the king sent for the parents of the hen, and told them they must repay to the hawk the amount of dowry they had received from him on the marriage of their daughter, according to the native custom; but the hen's parents said that they were so poor that they could not possibly afford to pay. So the king told the hawk that he could kill and eat any of the cock's children whenever and wherever he found them as payment of his dowry, and, if the cock made any complaint, the king would not listen to him.

From that time until now, whenever a hawk sees a chicken he swoops down and carries it off in part-payment of his dowry.

[64]

XVI

Why the Sun and the Moon live in the Sky

Many years ago the sun and water were great friends, and both lived on the earth together. The sun very often used to visit the water, but the water never returned his visits. At last the sun asked the water why it was that he never came to see him in his house, the water replied that the sun's house was not big enough, and that if he came with his people he would drive the sun out.

He then said, "If you wish me to visit you, you must build a very large compound; but I warn you that it will have to be a tremendous place, as my people are very numerous, and take up a lot of room."

The sun promised to build a very big compound, and soon afterwards he returned home to his wife, the moon, who greeted him with a broad smile when he opened the door. The sun told the moon what he had promised the water, and the next day commenced building a huge compound in which to entertain his friend.

When it was completed, he asked the water to come and visit him the next day.

When the water arrived, he called out to the sun, and asked him whether it would be safe for him[65] to enter, and the sun answered, "Yes, come in, my friend."

The water then began to flow in, accompanied by the fish and all the water animals.

Very soon the water was knee-deep, so he asked the sun if it was still safe, and the sun again said, "Yes," so more water came in.

When the water was level with the top of a man's head, the water said to the sun, "Do you want more of my people to come?" and the sun and moon both answered, "Yes," not knowing any better, so the water flowed on, until the sun and moon had to perch themselves on the top of the roof.

Again the water addressed the sun, but receiving the same answer, and more of his people rushing in, the water very soon overflowed the top of the roof, and the sun and moon were forced to go up into the sky, where they have remained ever since.

[66]

XVII

Why the Flies Bother the Cows

When Adiaha Umo was Queen of Calabar, being very rich and hospitable, she used to give big feasts to all the domestic animals, but never invited the wild beasts, as she was afraid of them.

At one feast she gave there were three large tables, and she told the cow to sit at the head of the table, as she was the biggest animal present, and share out the food. The cow was quite ready to do this, and the first course was passed, which the cow shared out amongst the people, but forgot the fly, because he was so small.

When the fly saw this, he called out to the cow to give him his share, but the cow said: "Be quiet, my friend, you must have patience."

When the second course arrived, the fly again called out to the cow, but the cow merely pointed to her eye, and told the fly to look there, and he would get food later.

At last all the dishes were finished, and the fly, having been given no food by the cow, went supperless to bed.

The next day the fly complained to the queen, who decided that, as the cow had presided at the feast, and had not given the fly his share, but had[67] pointed to her eye, for the future the fly could always get his food from the cow's eyes wherever she went; and even at the present time, wherever the cows are, the flies can always be seen feeding off their eyes in accordance with the queen's orders.

---

[68]

XVIII

Why the Cat kills Rats

Ansa was King of Calabar for fifty years. He had a very faithful cat as a housekeeper, and a rat was his house-boy. The king was an obstinate, headstrong man, but was very fond of the cat, who had been in his store for many years.

48

The rat, who was very poor, fell in love with one of the king's servant girls, but was unable to give her any presents, as he had no money.

At last he thought of the king's store, so in the night-time, being quite small, he had little difficulty, having made a hole in the roof, in getting into the store. He then stole corn and native pears, and presented them to his sweetheart.

At the end of the month, when the cat had to render her account of the things in the store to the king, it was found that a lot of corn and native pears were missing. The king was very angry at this, and asked the cat for an explanation. But the cat could not account for the loss, until one of her friends told her that the rat had been stealing the corn and giving it to the girl.

When the cat told the king, he called the girl before him and had her flogged. The rat he handed[69] over to the cat to deal with, and dismissed them both from his service. The cat was so angry at this that she killed and ate the rat, and ever since that time whenever a cat sees a rat she kills and eats it.

---

[70]

XIX

The Story of the Lightning and the Thunder

In the olden days the thunder and lightning lived on the earth amongst all the other people, but the king made them live at the far end of the town, as far as possible from other people's houses.

The thunder was an old mother sheep, and the lightning was her son, a ram. Whenever the ram got angry he used to go about and burn houses and knock down trees; he even did damage on the farms, and sometimes killed people. Whenever the lightning did these things, his mother used to call out to him in a very loud voice to stop and not to do any more damage; but the lightning did not care in the least for what his mother said, and when he was in a bad temper used to do a very large amount of damage. At last the people could not stand it any longer, and complained to the king.

So the king made a special order that the sheep (Thunder) and her son, the ram (Lightning), should leave the town and live in the far bush. This did not do much

49

good, as when the ram got angry he still burnt the forest, and the flames sometimes spread to the farms and consumed them.

So the people complained again, and the king banished both the lightning and the thunder from[71] the earth and made them live in the sky, where they could not cause so much destruction. Ever since, when the lightning is angry, he commits damage as before, but you can hear his mother, the thunder, rebuking him and telling him to stop. Sometimes, however, when the mother has gone away some distance from her naughty son, you can still see that he is angry and is doing damage, but his mother's voice cannot be heard.

---

[72]

XX

Why the Bush Cow and the Elephant are bad Friends

The bush cow and the elephant were always bad friends, and as they could not settle their disputes between themselves, they agreed to let the head chief decide.

The cause of their unfriendliness was that the elephant was always boasting about his strength to all his friends, which made the bush cow ashamed of himself, as he was always a good fighter and feared no man or animal. When the matter was referred to the head chief, he decided that the best way to settle the dispute was for the elephant and bush cow to meet and fight one another in a large open space. He decided that the fight should take place in the market-place on the next market-day, when all the country people could witness the battle.

When the market-day arrived, the bush cow went out in the early morning and took up his position some distance from the town on the main road to the market, and started bellowing and tearing up the ground. As the people passed he asked them whether they had seen anything of the "Big, Big one," which was the name of the elephant.[73]

A bush buck, who happened to be passing, replied, "I am only a small antelope, and am on my way to the market. How should I know anything of the movements of the 'Big, Big one?'" The bush cow then allowed him to pass.

After a little time the bush cow heard the elephant trumpeting, and could hear him as he came nearer breaking down trees and trampling down the small bush.

When the elephant came near the bush cow, they both charged one another, and a tremendous fight commenced, in which a lot of damage was done to the surrounding farms, and many of the people were frightened to go to the market, and returned to their houses.

At last the monkey, who had been watching the fight from a distance whilst he was jumping from branch to branch high up in the trees, thought he would report what he had seen to the head chief. Although he forgot several times what it was he wanted to do, which is a little way monkeys have, he eventually reached the chief's house, and jumped upon the roof, where he caught and ate a spider. He then climbed to the ground again, and commenced playing with a small stick. But he very soon got tired of this, and then, picking up a stone, he rubbed it backwards and forwards on the ground in an aimless sort of way, whilst looking in the opposite direction. This did not last long, and very soon he was busily engaged in a minute personal inspection.

His attention was then attracted by a large praying mantis, which had fluttered into the house, making[74] much clatter with its wings. When it settled, it immediately assumed its usual prayerful attitude.

The monkey, after a careful stalk, seized the mantis, and having deliberately pulled the legs off one after the other, he ate the body, and sat down with his head on one side, looking very wise, but in reality thinking of nothing.

Just then the chief caught sight of him while he was scratching himself, and shouted out in a loud voice, "Ha, monkey, is that you? What do you want here?"

At the chief's voice the monkey gave a jump, and started chattering like anything. After a time he replied very nervously: "Oh yes, of course! Yes, I came to see you." Then he said to himself, "I wonder what on earth it was I came to tell the chief?" but it was no use, everything had gone out of his head.

Then the chief told the monkey he might take one of the ripe plantains hanging up in the verandah. The monkey did not want telling twice, as he was very fond of plantains. He soon tore off the skin, and holding the plantain in both hands, took bite after bite from the end of it, looking at it carefully after each bite.

Then the chief remarked that the elephant and the bush cow ought to have arrived by that time, as they were going to have a great fight. Directly the monkey heard this he remembered what it was he wanted to tell the chief; so, having swallowed the piece of plantain he had placed in the side of his cheek, he said: "Ah! that reminds me," and then, after much chattering and making all sorts of funny grimaces,[75] finally made the chief understand that the elephant and bush cow, instead of fighting where they had been told, were having it out in the bush on the main road leading to the market, and had thus stopped most of the people coming in.

When the chief heard this he was much incensed, and called for his bow and poisoned arrows, and went to the scene of the combat. He then shot both the elephant and the bush cow, and throwing his bow and arrows away, ran and hid himself in the bush. About six hours afterwards both the elephant and bush cow died in great pain.

Ever since, when wild animals want to fight between themselves, they always fight in the big bush and not on the public roads; but as the fight was never definitely decided between the elephant and the bush cow, whenever they meet one another in the forest, even to the present time, they always fight.

---

[76]

XXI

The Cock who caused a Fight between two Towns

Ekpo and Etim were half-brothers, that is to say they had the same mother, but different fathers. Their mother first of all had married a chief of Duke Town, when Ekpo was born; but after a time she got tired of him and went to Old Town, where she married Ejuqua and gave birth to Etim.

Both of the boys grew up and became very rich. Ekpo had a cock, of which he was very fond, and every day when Ekpo sat down to meals the cock used to fly on to the table and feed also. Ama Ukwa, a native of Old Town, who was rather poor, was jealous of the two brothers, and made up his mind if possible to bring about a quarrel between them, although he pretended to be friends with both.

One day Ekpo, the elder brother, gave a big dinner, to which Etim and many other people were invited. Ama Ukwa was also present. A very good dinner was laid for the guests, and plenty of palm wine was provided. When they had commenced to feed, the pet cock flew on to the table and began to feed off Etim's plate. Etim then told one of his servants to seize the cock and tie him up in the[77] house until after the feast. So the servant carried the cock to Etim's house and tied him up for safety.

After much eating and drinking, Etim returned home late at night with his friend Ama Ukwa, and just before they went to bed, Ama Ukwa saw Ekpo's cock tied up. So early in the morning he went to Ekpo's house, who received him gladly.

About eight o'clock, when it was time for Ekpo to have his early morning meal, he noticed that his pet cock was missing. When he remarked upon its absence, Ama Ukwa told him that his brother had seized the cock the previous evening during the dinner, and was going to kill it, just to see what Ekpo would do. When Ekpo heard this, he was very vexed, and sent Ama Ukwa back to his brother to ask him to return the cock immediately. Instead of delivering the message as he had been instructed, Ama Ukwa told Etim that his elder brother was so angry with him for taking away his friend, the cock, that he would fight him, and had sent Ama Ukwa on purpose to declare war between the two towns.

Etim then told Ama Ukwa to return to Ekpo, and say he would be prepared for anything his brother could do. Ama Ukwa then advised Ekpo to call all his people in from their farms, as Etim would attack him, and on his return he advised Etim to do the same. He then arranged a day for the fight to take place between the two brothers and their people. Etim then marched his men to the other side of the creek, and waited for his brother; so Ama Ukwa went to Ekpo and told him that Etim had got all his people together and was waiting to fight. Ekpo then led his men against his brother,[78] and there was a big battle, many men being killed on both sides. The fighting went on all day, until at last, towards evening, the other chiefs of Calabar met and determined to stop it; so they called the Egbo men together and sent them out with their drums, and eventually the fight stopped.

Three days later a big palaver was held, when each of the brothers was told to state his case. When they had done so, it was found that Ama Ukwa had caused the quarrel, and the chiefs ordered that he should be killed. His father, who was a rich man, offered to give the Egbos five thousand rods, five cows, and seven slaves to redeem his son, but they decided to refuse his offer.

The next day, after being severely flogged, he was left for twenty-four hours tied up to a tree, and the following day his head was cut off.

Ekpo was then ordered to kill his pet cock, so that it should not cause any further trouble between himself and his brother, and a law was passed that for the future no one should keep a pet cock or any other tame animal.

[79]

XXII

The Affair of the Hippopotamus and the Tortoise; or, Why the Hippopotamus lives in the Water

Many years ago the hippopotamus, whose name was Isantim, was one of the biggest kings on the land; he was second only to the elephant. The hippo had seven large fat wives, of whom he was very fond. Now and then he used to give a big feast to the people, but a curious thing was that, although everyone knew the hippo, no one, except his seven wives, knew his name.

At one of the feasts, just as the people were about to sit down, the hippo said, "You have come to feed at my table, but none of you know my name. If you cannot tell my name, you shall all of you go away without your dinner."

As they could not guess his name, they had to go away and leave all the good food and tombo behind them. But before they left, the tortoise stood up and asked the hippopotamus what he would do if he told him his name at the next feast? So the hippo replied that he would be so ashamed of himself, that he and his whole family would leave the land, and for the future would dwell in the water. [80]

Now it was the custom for the hippo and his seven wives to go down every morning and evening to the river to wash and have a drink. Of this custom the tortoise was aware. The hippo used to walk first, and the seven wives followed. One day when they had gone down to the river to bathe, the tortoise made a small hole in the middle of the path, and then waited. When the hippo and his wives returned, two of the wives were some distance behind, so the tortoise came out from where he had been hiding, and half buried himself in the hole he had dug, leaving the greater part of his shell exposed. When the two hippo wives came along, the first one knocked her foot against the tortoise's shell, and immediately called out to her husband, "Oh! Isantim, my husband, I have hurt my foot." At this the tortoise was very glad, and went joyfully home, as he had found out the hippo's name.

When the next feast was given by the hippo, he made the same condition about his name; so the tortoise got up and said, "You promise you will not kill me if I tell you your name?" and the hippo promised. The tortoise then shouted as loud as he was able, "Your name is Isantim," at which a cheer went up from all the people, and then they sat down to their dinner.

When the feast was over, the hippo, with his seven wives, in accordance with his promise, went down to the river, and they have always lived in the water from that day till now; and although they come on shore to feed at night, you never find a hippo on the land in the daytime.

[81]

XXIII

Why Dead People are Buried

In the beginning of the world when the Creator had made men and women and the animals, they all lived together in the creation land. The Creator was a big chief, past all men, and being very kind-hearted, was very sorry whenever anyone died. So one day he sent for the dog, who was his head messenger, and told him to go out into the world and give his word to all people that for the future whenever anyone died the body was to be placed in the compound, and wood ashes were to be thrown over it; that the dead body was to be left on the ground, and in twenty-four hours it would become alive again.

When the dog had travelled for half a day he began to get tired; so as he was near an old woman's house he looked in, and seeing a bone with some meat on it he made a meal off it, and then went to sleep, entirely forgetting the message which had been given him to deliver.

After a time, when the dog did not return, the Creator called for a sheep, and sent him out with the same message. But the sheep was a very foolish one, and being hungry, began eating the sweet grasses by the wayside. After a time, however,[82] he remembered that he had a message to deliver, but forgot what it was exactly; so as he went about among the people he told them that the message the Creator had given him to tell the people, was that whenever anyone died they should be buried underneath the ground.

A little time afterwards the dog remembered his message, so he ran into the town and told the people that they were to place wood ashes on the dead bodies and leave them in the compound, and that they would come to life again after twenty-four hours. But the people would not believe him, and said, "We have already received the word from the Creator by the sheep, that all dead bodies should be buried." In consequence of this the dead bodies are now always buried, and the dog is much disliked and not trusted as a messenger, as if he had not found the bone in the old woman's house and forgotten his message, the dead people might still be alive.

---

[83]

XXIV

Of the Fat Woman who Melted Away

There was once a very fat woman who was made of oil. She was very beautiful, and many young men applied to the parents for permission to marry their daughter, and offered dowry, but the mother always refused, as she said it was impossible for her daughter to work on a farm, as she would melt in the sun. At last a stranger came from a far-distant country and fell in love with the fat woman, and he promised if her mother would hand her to him that he would keep her in the shade. At last the mother agreed, and he took his wife away.

When he arrived at his house, his other wife immediately became very jealous, because when there was work to be done, firewood to be collected, or water to be carried, the fat woman stayed at home and never helped, as she was frightened of the heat.

One day when the husband was absent, the jealous wife abused the fat woman so much that she finally agreed to go and work on the farm, although her little sister, whom she had brought from home with her, implored her not to go, reminding her that their mother had always told them ever since they were born that she would melt away[84] if she went into the sun. All the way to the farm the fat woman managed to keep in the shade, and when they arrived at the farm the sun was very hot, so the fat woman remained in the shade of a big tree. When the jealous wife saw this she again began abusing her, and asked her why she did not do her share of the work. At last she could stand the nagging no longer, and although her little sister tried very hard to prevent her, the fat woman went out into the sun to work, and immediately began to melt away. There was very soon nothing left of her but one big toe, which had been covered by a leaf. This her little sister observed, and with tears in her eyes she picked up the toe, which was all that remained of the fat woman, and having covered it carefully with leaves, placed it in the bottom of her basket. When she arrived at the house the little sister placed the toe in an earthen pot, filled it with water, and covered the top up with clay.

When the husband returned, he said, "Where is my fat wife?" and the little sister, crying bitterly, told him that the jealous woman had made her go out into the sun, and that she had melted away. She then showed him the pot with the remains of her sister, and told him that her sister would come to life again in three months' time quite complete, but he must send away the jealous wife, so that there should be no more trouble; if he refused to do this, the little girl said she would take the pot back to their mother, and when her sister became complete again they would remain at home.

The husband then took the jealous wife back to her parents, who sold her as a slave and paid the[85] dowry back to the husband, so that he could get another wife. When he received the money, the husband took it home and kept it until the three months had elapsed, when the little sister opened the pot and the fat woman emerged, quite as fat and beautiful as she had been before. The husband was so delighted that he gave a feast to all his friends and neighbours, and told them the whole story of the bad behaviour of his jealous wife.

Ever since that time, whenever a wife behaves very badly the husband returns her to the parents, who sell the woman as a slave, and out of the proceeds of the sale reimburse the husband the amount of dowry which he paid when he married the girl.

---

[86]

XXV

Concerning the Leopard, the Squirrel, and the Tortoise

Many years ago there was a great famine throughout the land, and all the people were starving. The yam crop had failed entirely, the plantains did not bear any fruit, the ground-nuts were all shrivelled up, and the corn never came to a head; even the palm-oil nuts did not ripen, and the peppers and ocros also gave out.

The leopard, however, who lived entirely on "beef," did not care for any of these things; and although some of the animals who lived on corn and the growing crops began to get rather skinny, he did not mind very much. In order to save himself trouble, as everybody was complaining of the famine, he called a meeting of all the animals and told them that, as they all knew, he was very powerful and must have food, that the famine did not affect him, as he only lived on flesh, and as there were plenty of animals about he did not intend to starve. He then told all the animals present at the meeting that if they did not wish to be killed themselves they must bring their grandmothers to him for food, and when they were finished he would feed off their mothers. The animals might[87] bring their grandmothers in succession, and he would take them in their turn; so that, as there were many different animals, it would probably be some time before their mothers were eaten, by which time it was possible that the famine would be over. But in any case, he warned them that he was determined to have sufficient food for himself, and that if the grandmothers or mothers were not forthcoming he would turn upon the young people themselves and kill and eat them.

This, of course, the young generation, who had attended the meeting, did not appreciate, and in order to save their own skins, agreed to supply the leopard with his daily meal.

The first to appear with his aged grandmother was the squirrel. The grandmother was a poor decrepit old thing, with a mangy tail, and the leopard swallowed her at one gulp, and then looked round for more. In an angry voice he growled out: "This is not the proper food for me; I must have more at once."

Then a bush cat pushed his old grandmother in front of the leopard, but he snarled at her and said, "Take the nasty old thing away; I want some sweet food."

It was then the turn of a bush buck, and after a great deal of hesitation a wretchedly poor and thin old doe tottered and fell in front of the leopard, who immediately despatched her, and although the meal was very unsatisfactory, declared that his appetite was appeased for that day.

The next day a few more animals brought their old grandmothers, until at last it became the tortoise'[88]s turn; but being very cunning, he produced witnesses to prove that his grandmother was dead, so the leopard excused him.

After a few days all the animals' grandmothers were exhausted, and it became the turn of the mothers to supply food for the ravenous leopard. Now although most of the young animals did not mind getting rid of their grandmothers, whom they had scarcely even known, many of them had very strong objections to providing their mothers, of whom they were very fond, as food for the leopard. Amongst the strongest objectors were the squirrel and the tortoise. The tortoise, who had thought the whole thing out, was aware that, as everyone knew that his mother was alive (she being rather an amiable old person and friendly with all-comers), the same excuse would not avail him a second time. He therefore told his mother to climb up a palm tree, and that he would provide her with food until the famine was over. He instructed her to let down a basket every day, and said that he would place food in it for her. The tortoise made the basket for his mother, and attached it to a long string of tie-tie. The string was so strong that she could haul her son up whenever he wished to visit her.

All went well for some days, as the tortoise used to go at daylight to the bottom of the tree where his mother lived and place her food in the basket; then the old lady would pull the basket up and have her food, and the tortoise would depart on his daily round in his usual leisurely manner.

In the meantime the leopard had to have his daily food, and the squirrel's turn came first after the[89] grandmothers had been finished, so he was forced to produce his mother for the leopard to eat, as he was a poor, weak thing and not possessed of any cunning. The squirrel was, however, very fond of his mother, and when she had been eaten he remembered that the tortoise had not produced his grandmother for the leopard's food. He therefore determined to set a watch on the movements of the tortoise.

The very next morning, while he was gathering nuts, he saw the tortoise walking very slowly through the bush, and being high up in the trees and able to travel very fast, had no difficulty in keeping the tortoise in sight without being noticed. When the tortoise arrived at the foot of the tree where his mother lived, he placed the food in the basket which his mother had let down already by the tie-tie, and having got into the basket and given a pull at the string to signify that everything was right, was hauled up, and after a time was let down again in the basket. The squirrel was watching all the time, and directly the tortoise had gone, jumped from branch to branch of the trees, and very soon arrived at the place where the leopard was snoozing.

When he woke up, the squirrel said:

"You have eaten my grandmother and my mother, but the tortoise has not provided any food for you. It is now his turn, and he has hidden his mother away in a tree."

At this the leopard was very angry, and told the squirrel to lead him at once to the tree where the tortoise's mother lived. But the squirrel said:

"The tortoise only goes at daylight, when his[90] mother lets down a basket; so if you go in the morning early, she will pull you up, and you can then kill her."

To this the leopard agreed, and the next morning the squirrel came at cockcrow and led the leopard to the tree where the tortoise's mother was hidden. The old lady had already let down the basket for her daily supply of food, and the leopard got into it and gave the line a pull; but except a few small jerks nothing happened, as the old mother tortoise was not strong enough to pull a heavy leopard off the ground. When the leopard saw that he was not going to be pulled up, being an expert climber, he scrambled up the tree, and when he got to the top he found the poor old tortoise, whose shell was so tough that he thought she was not worth eating, so he threw her down on to the ground in a violent temper, and then came down himself and went home.

Shortly after this the tortoise arrived at the tree, and finding the basket on the ground gave his usual tug at it, but there was no answer. He then looked about, and after a little time came upon the broken shell of his poor old mother, who by this time was quite dead. The tortoise knew at once that the leopard had killed his mother, and made up his mind that for the future he would live alone and have nothing to do with the other animals.

[91]

XXVI

Why the Moon Waxes and Wanes

There was once an old woman who was very poor, and lived in a small mud hut thatched with mats made from the leaves of the tombo palm in the bush. She was often very hungry, as there was no one to look after her.

In the olden days the moon used often to come down to the earth, although she lived most of the time in the sky. The moon was a fat woman with a skin of hide, and she was full of fat meat. She was quite round, and in the night used to give plenty of light. The moon was sorry for the poor starving old woman, so she came to her and said, "You may cut some of my meat away for your food." This the old woman did every evening, and the moon got smaller and smaller until you could scarcely see her at all. Of course this made her give very little light, and all the people began to grumble in consequence, and to ask why it was that the moon was getting so thin.

At last the people went to the old woman's house where there happened to be a little girl sleeping. She had been there for some little time, and had seen the moon come down every evening, and the old woman go out with her knife and carve her[92] daily supply of meat out of the moon. As she was very frightened, she told the people all about it, so they determined to set a watch on the movements of the old woman.

That very night the moon came down as usual, and the old woman went out with her knife and basket to get her food; but before she could carve any meat all the people rushed out shouting, and the moon was so frightened that she went back again into the sky, and never came down again to the earth. The old woman was left to starve in the bush.

Ever since that time the moon has hidden herself most of the day, as she was so frightened, and she still gets very thin once a month, but later on she gets fat again, and when she is quite fat she gives plenty of light all the night; but this does not last very long, and she begins to get thinner and thinner, in the same way as she did when the old woman was carving her meat from her.

---

[93]

XXVII

The Story of the Leopard, the Tortoise, and the Bush Rat

At the time of the great famine all the animals were very thin and weak from want of food; but there was one exception, and that was the tortoise and all his family, who were quite fat, and did not seem to suffer at all. Even the leopard was very thin, in spite of the arrangement he had made with the animals to bring him their old grandmothers and mothers for food.

In the early days of the famine (as you will remember) the leopard had killed the mother of the tortoise, in consequence of which the tortoise was very angry with the leopard, and determined if possible to be revenged upon him. The tortoise, who was very clever, had discovered a shallow lake full of fish in the middle of the forest, and every morning he used to go to the lake and, without much trouble, bring back enough food for himself and his family. One day the leopard met the tortoise and noticed how fat he was. As he was very thin himself he decided to watch the tortoise, so the next morning he hid himself in the long grass near the tortoise's house and waited very patiently, until at last the tortoise came along quite slowly, carrying a basket[94] which appeared to be very heavy. Then the leopard sprang out, and said to the tortoise:

"What have you got in that basket?"

The tortoise, as he did not want to lose his breakfast, replied that he was carrying firewood back to his home. Unfortunately for the tortoise the leopard had a very acute sense of smell, and knew at once that there was fish in the basket, so he said:

"I know there is fish in there, and I am going to eat it."

The tortoise, not being in a position to refuse, as he was such a poor creature, said:

"Very well. Let us sit down under this shady tree, and if you will make a fire I will go to my house and get pepper, oil, and salt, and then we will feed together."

To this the leopard agreed, and began to search about for dry wood, and started the fire. In the meantime the tortoise waddled off to his house, and very soon returned with the pepper, salt, and oil; he also brought a long piece of cane tie-tie, which is very strong. This he put on the ground, and began boiling the fish. Then he said to the leopard:

"While we are waiting for the fish to cook, let us play at tying one another up to a tree. You may tie me up first, and when I say 'Tighten,' you must loose the rope, and when I say 'Loosen,' you must tighten the rope."

The leopard, who was very hungry, thought that this game would make the time pass more quickly until the fish was cooked, so he said he would play. The tortoise then stood with his back to the tree [95] and said, "Loosen the rope," and the leopard, in accordance with the rules of the game, began to tie up the tortoise. Very soon the tortoise shouted out, "Tighten!" and the leopard at once unfastened the tie-tie, and the tortoise was free. The tortoise then said, "Now, leopard, it is your turn;" so the leopard stood up against the tree and called out to the tortoise to loosen the rope, and the tortoise at once very quickly passed the rope several times round the leopard and got him fast to the tree. Then the leopard said, "Tighten the rope;" but instead of playing the game in accordance with the rules he had laid down, the tortoise ran faster and faster with the rope round the leopard, taking great care, however, to keep out of reach of the leopard's claws, and very soon had the leopard so securely fastened that it was quite impossible for him to free himself.

All this time the leopard was calling out to the tortoise to let him go, as he was tired of the game; but the tortoise only laughed, and sat down at the fireside and commenced his meal. When he had finished he packed up the remainder of the fish for his family, and prepared to go, but before he started he said to the leopard:

"You killed my mother and now you want to take my fish. It is not likely that I am going to the lake to get fish for you, so I shall leave you here to starve."

He then threw the remains of the pepper and salt into the leopard's eyes and quietly went on his way, leaving the leopard roaring with pain.

All that day and throughout the night the leopard was calling out for some one to release him, and[96] vowing all sorts of vengeance on the tortoise; but no one came, as the people and animals of the forest do not like to hear the leopard's voice.

In the morning, when the animals began to go about to get their food, the leopard called out to every one he saw to come and untie him, but they all refused, as they knew that if they did so the leopard would most likely kill them at once and eat them. At last a bush rat came near and saw the leopard tied up to the tree and asked him what was the matter, so the leopard told him that he had been playing a game of "tight" and "loose" with the tortoise, and that he had tied him up and left him there to starve. The leopard then implored the bush rat to cut the ropes with his sharp teeth. The bush rat was very sorry for the leopard; but at the same time he knew that, if he let the leopard go, he would most likely be killed and eaten, so he hesitated, and said that he did not quite see his way to cutting the ropes. But this bush rat, being rather kind-hearted, and having had some experience of traps himself, could sympathise with the leopard in his uncomfortable position. He therefore thought for a time, and then hit upon a plan. He first started to dig a hole under the tree, quite regardless of the leopard's cries. When he had finished the hole he came out and cut one of the ropes, and immediately ran into his hole, and waited there to see what would happen; but although the leopard struggled frantically, he could not get loose, as the tortoise had tied him up so fast. After a time, when he saw that there was no danger, the bush rat crept out again and very carefully bit through another rope, and then retired to his hole as[97] before. Again nothing happened, and he began to feel more confidence, so he bit several strands through one after the other until at last the leopard was free. The leopard, who was ravenous with hunger, instead of being grateful to the bush rat, directly he was free, made a dash at the bush rat with his big paw, but just missed him, as the bush rat had dived for his hole; but he was not quite quick enough to escape altogether, and the leopard's sharp claws scored his back and left marks which he carried to his grave.

Ever since then the bush rats have had white spots on their skins, which represent the marks of the leopard's claws.

[98]

XXVIII

The King and the Ju Ju Tree

Udo Ubok Udom was a famous king who lived at Itam, which is an inland town, and does not possess a river. The king and his wife therefore used to wash at the spring just behind their house.

King Udo had a daughter, of whom he was very fond, and looked after her most carefully, and she grew up into a beautiful woman.

For some time the king had been absent from his house, and had not been to the spring for two years. When he went to his old place to wash, he found that the Idem Ju Ju tree had grown up all round the place, and it was impossible for him to use the spring as he had done formerly. He therefore called fifty of his young men to bring their matchets[8] and cut down the tree. They started cutting the tree, but it had no effect, as, directly they made a cut in the tree, it closed up again; so, after working all day, they found they had made no impression on it.

When they returned at night, they told the king that they had been unable to destroy the tree. He [99]was very angry when he heard this, and went to the spring the following morning, taking his own matchet with him.

When the Ju Ju tree saw that the king had come himself and was starting to try to cut his branches, he caused a small splinter of wood to go into the king's eye. This gave the king great pain, so he threw down his matchet and went back to his house. The pain, however, got worse, and he could not eat or sleep for three days.

He therefore sent for his witch men, and told them to cast lots to find out why he was in such pain. When they had cast lots, they decided that the reason was that the Ju Ju tree was angry with the king because he wanted to wash at the spring, and had tried to destroy the tree.

They then told the king that he must take seven baskets of flies, a white goat, a white chicken, and a piece of white cloth, and make a sacrifice of them in order to satisfy the Ju Ju.

The king did this, and the witch men tried their lotions on the king's eye, but it got worse and worse.

He then dismissed these witches and got another lot. When they arrived they told the king that, although they could do nothing themselves to relieve his pain, they knew

64

one man who lived in the spirit land who could cure him; so the king told them to send for him at once, and he arrived the next day.

Then the spirit man said, "Before I do anything to your eye, what will you give me?" So King Udo said, "I will give you half my town with the people in it, also seven cows and some money." But the[100] spirit man refused to accept the king's offer. As the king was in such pain, he said, "Name your own price, and I will pay you." So the spirit man said the only thing he was willing to accept as payment was the king's daughter. At this the king cried very much, and told the man to go away, as he would rather die than let him have his daughter.

That night the pain was worse than ever, and some of his subjects pleaded with the king to send for the spirit man again and give him his daughter, and told him that when he got well he could no doubt have another daughter but that if he died now he would lose everything.

The king then sent for the spirit man again, who came very quickly, and in great grief the king handed his daughter to the spirit.

The spirit man then went out into the bush, and collected some leaves, which he soaked in water and beat up. The juice he poured into the king's eye, and told him that when he washed his face in the morning he would be able to see what was troubling him in the eye.

The king tried to persuade him to stay the night, but the spirit man refused, and departed that same night for the spirit land, taking the king's daughter with him.

Before it was light the king rose up and washed his face, and found that the small splinter from the Ju Ju tree, which had been troubling him so much, dropped out of his eye, the pain disappeared, and he was quite well again.

When he came to his proper senses he realised[101] that he had sacrificed his daughter for one of his eyes, so he made an order that there should be general mourning throughout his kingdom for three years.

For the first two years of the mourning the king's daughter was put in the fatting house by the spirit man, and was given food; but a skull, who was in the house, told her not to eat, as they were fatting her up, not for marriage, but so that they could eat her. She therefore gave all the food which was brought to her to the skull, and lived on chalk herself.

Towards the end of the third year the spirit man brought some of his friends to see the king's daughter, and told them he would kill her the next day, and they would have a good feast off her.

When she woke up in the morning the spirit man brought her food as usual; but the skull, who wanted to preserve her life, and who had heard what the spirit man had said, called her into the room and told her what was going to happen later in the day. She handed the food to the skull, and he said, "When the spirit man goes to the wood with his friends to prepare for the feast, you must run back to your father."

He then gave her some medicine which would make her strong for the journey, and also gave her directions as to the road, telling her that there were two roads but that when she came to the parting of the ways she was to drop some of the medicine on the ground and the two roads would become one.

He then told her to leave by the back door, and go through the wood until she came to the end[102] of the town; she would then find the road. If she met people on the road she was to pass them in silence, as if she saluted them they would know that she was a stranger in the spirit land, and might kill her. She was also not to turn round if any one called to her, but was to go straight on till she reached her father's house.

Having thanked the skull for his kind advice, the king's daughter started off, and when she reached the end of the town and found the road, she ran for three hours, and at last arrived at the branch roads. There she dropped the medicine, as she had been instructed, and the two roads immediately became one; so she went straight on and never saluted any one or turned back, although several people called to her.

About this time the spirit man had returned from the wood, and went to the house, only to find the king's daughter was absent. He asked the skull where she was, and he replied that she had gone out by the back door, but he did not know where she had gone to. Being a spirit, however, he very soon guessed that she had gone home; so he followed as quickly as possible, shouting out all the time.

When the girl heard his voice she ran as fast as she could, and at last arrived at her father's house, and told him to take at once a cow, a pig, a sheep, a goat, a dog, a chicken, and seven eggs, and cut them into seven parts as a sacrifice, and leave them on the road, so that when the spirit man saw these things he would stop and not enter the town. This the king did immediately, and made the sacrifice as his daughter had told him.[103]

When the spirit man saw the sacrifice on the road, he sat down and at once began to eat.

When he had satisfied his appetite, he packed up the remainder and returned to the spirit land, not troubling any more about the king's daughter.

When the king saw that the danger was over, he beat his drum, and declared that for the future, when people died and went to the spirit land, they should not come to earth again as spirits to cure sick people.

FOOTNOTES

[8]A matchet is a long sharp knife in general use throughout the country. It has a wooden handle; it is about two feet six inches long and two inches wide.

---

[104]

XXIX

How the Tortoise overcame the Elephant and the Hippopotamus

The elephant and the hippopotamus always used to feed together, and were good friends.

One day when they were both dining together, the tortoise appeared and said that although they were both big and strong, neither of them could pull him out of the water with a strong piece of tie-tie, and he offered the elephant ten thousand rods if he could draw him out of the river the next day. The elephant, seeing that the tortoise was very small, said, "If I cannot draw you out of the water, I will give you twenty thousand rods." So on the following morning the tortoise got some very strong tie-tie and made it fast to his leg, and went down to the river. When he got there, as he knew the place well, he made the tie-tie fast round a big rock, and left the other end on the shore for the elephant to pull by, then went down to the bottom of the river and hid himself. The elephant then came down and started pulling, and after a time he smashed the rope.

Directly this happened, the tortoise undid the rope from the rock and came to the land, showing all people that the rope was still fast to his leg, but[105] that the elephant had failed to pull him out. The elephant was thus forced to admit that the tortoise was the winner, and paid to him the twenty thousand rods, as agreed. The tortoise then took the rods home to his wife, and they lived together very happily.

After three months had passed, the tortoise, seeing that the money was greatly reduced, thought he would make some more by the same trick, so he went to the hippopotamus and made the same bet with him. The hippopotamus said, "I will make

67

the bet, but I shall take the water and you shall take the land; I will then pull you into the water."

To this the tortoise agreed, so they went down to the river as before, and having got some strong tie-tie, the tortoise made it fast to the hippopotamus' hind leg, and told him to go into the water. Directly the hippo had turned his back and disappeared, the tortoise took the rope twice round a strong palm-tree which was growing near, and then hid himself at the foot of the tree.

When the hippo was tired of pulling, he came up puffing and blowing water into the air from his nostrils. Directly the tortoise saw him coming up, he unwound the rope, and walked down towards the hippopotamus, showing him the tie-tie round his leg. The hippo had to acknowledge that the tortoise was too strong for him, and reluctantly handed over the twenty thousand rods.

The elephant and the hippo then agreed that they would take the tortoise as their friend, as he was so very strong; but he was not really so strong as they thought, and had won because he was so cunning.

He then told them that he would like to live with[106] both of them, but that, as he could not be in two places at the same time, he said that he would leave his son to live with the elephant on the land, and that he himself would live with the hippopotamus in the water.

This explains why there are both tortoises on the land and tortoises who live in the water. The water tortoise is always much the bigger of the two, as there is plenty of fish for him to eat in the river, whereas the land tortoise is often very short of food.

[107]

XXX

Of the Pretty Girl and the Seven Jealous Women

There was once a very beautiful girl called Akim. She was a native of Ibibio, and the name was given to her on account of her good looks, as she was born in the spring-time. She was an only daughter, and her parents were extremely fond of her. The people of the town, and more particularly the young girls, were so jealous of Akim's good looks and beautiful form—for she was perfectly made, very strong, and her

68

carriage, bearing, and manners were most graceful—that her parents would not allow her to join the young girls' society in the town, as is customary for all young people to do, both boys and girls belonging to a company according to their age; a company consisting, as a rule, of all the boys or girls born in the same year.

Akim's parents were rather poor, but she was a good daughter, and gave them no trouble, so they had a happy home. One day as Akim was on her way to draw water from the spring she met the company of seven girls, to which in an ordinary way she would have belonged, if her parents had not forbidden her. These girls told her that they were going to hold a play in the town in three days' time,[108] and asked her to join them. She said she was very sorry, but that her parents were poor, and only had herself to work for them, she therefore had no time to spare for dancing and plays. She then left them and went home.

In the evening the seven girls met together, and as they were very envious of Akim, they discussed how they should be revenged upon her for refusing to join their company, and they talked for a long time as to how they could get Akim into danger or punish her in some way.

At last one of the girls suggested that they should all go to Akim's house every day and help her with her work, so that when they had made friends with her they would be able to entice her away and take their revenge upon her for being more beautiful than themselves. Although they went every day and helped Akim and her parents with their work, the parents knew that they were jealous of their daughter, and repeatedly warned her not on any account to go with them, as they were not to be trusted.

At the end of the year there was going to be a big play, called the new yam play, to which Akim's parents had been invited. The play was going to be held at a town about two hours' march from where they lived. Akim was very anxious to go and take part in the dance, but her parents gave her plenty of work to do before they started, thinking that this would surely prevent her going, as she was a very obedient daughter, and always did her work properly.

On the morning of the play the jealous seven came to Akim and asked her to go with them, but she pointed to all the water-pots she had to fill, and[109] showed them where her parents had told her to polish the walls with a stone and make the floor good; and after that was finished she had to pull up all the weeds round the house and clean up all round. She therefore said it was impossible for her to leave the house until all the work was finished. When the girls heard this they took up the water-pots, went to the spring, and quickly returned with them full; they placed them in a row, and then they got stones, and very soon had the walls polished and the floor made good; after that they did the weeding outside and the cleaning up, and when everything was completed they said to Akim, "Now then, come along; you have no excuse to remain behind, as all the work is done."

Akim really wanted to go to the play; so as all the work was done which her parents had told her to do, she finally consented to go. About half-way to the town, where the new yam play was being held, there was a small river, about five feet deep, which had to be crossed by wading, as there was no bridge. In this river there was a powerful Ju Ju, whose law was that whenever anyone crossed the river and returned the same way on the return journey, whoever it was, had to give some food to the Ju Ju. If they did not make the proper sacrifice the Ju Ju dragged them down and took them to his home, and kept them there to work for him. The seven jealous girls knew all about this Ju Ju, having often crossed the river before, as they walked about all over the country, and had plenty of friends in the different towns. Akim, however, who was a good girl, and never went anywhere, knew nothing about this Ju Ju, which her companions had found out. [110]

When the work was finished they all started off together, and crossed the river without any trouble. When they had gone a small distance on the other side they saw a small bird, perched on a high tree, who admired Akim very much, and sang in praise of her beauty, much to the annoyance of the seven girls; but they walked on without saying anything, and eventually arrived at the town where the play was being held. Akim had not taken the trouble to change her clothes, but when she arrived at the town, although her companions had on all their best beads and their finest clothes, the young men and people admired Akim far more than the other girls, and she was declared to be the finest and most beautiful woman at the dance. They gave her plenty of palm wine, foo-foo, and everything she wanted, so that the seven girls became more angry and jealous than before. The people danced and sang all that night, but Akim managed to keep out of the sight of her parents until the following morning, when they asked her how it was that she had disobeyed them and neglected her work; so Akim told them that the work had all been done by her friends, and they had enticed her to come to the play with them. Her mother then told her to return home at once, and that she was not to remain in the town any longer.

When Akim told her friends this they said, "Very well, we are just going to have some small meal, and then we will return with you." They all then sat down together and had their food, but each of the seven jealous girls hid a small quantity of foo-foo and fish in her clothes for the Water Ju Ju. However Akim, who knew nothing about this, as her parents had[111] forgotten to tell her about the Ju Ju, never thinking for one moment that their daughter would cross the river, did not take any food as a sacrifice to the Ju Ju with her.

When they arrived at the river Akim saw the girls making their small sacrifices, and begged them to give her a small share so that she could do the same, but they refused, and all walked across the river safely. Then when it was Akim's turn to cross, when she arrived in the middle of the river, the Water Ju Ju caught hold of her and dragged her underneath the water, so that she immediately disappeared from sight. The seven girls had been watching for this, and when they saw that she had gone they went on their way, very pleased at the success of their scheme, and said to one another, "Now Akim is gone for ever, and we shall hear no more about her being better-looking than we are."

As there was no one to be seen at the time when Akim disappeared they naturally thought that their cruel action had escaped detection, so they went home rejoicing; but they never noticed the little bird high up in the tree who had sung of Akim's beauty when they were on their way to the play. The little bird was very sorry for Akim, and made up his mind that, when the proper time came, he would tell her parents what he had seen, so that perhaps they would be able to save her. The bird had heard Akim asking for a small portion of the food to make a sacrifice with, and had heard all the girls refusing to give her any.

The following morning, when Akim's parents returned[112] home, they were much surprised to find that the door was fastened, and that there was no sign of their daughter anywhere about the place, so they inquired of their neighbours, but no one was able to give them any information about her. They then went to the seven girls, and asked them what had become of Akim. They replied that they did not know what had become of her, but that she had reached their town safely with them, and then said she was going home. The father then went to his Ju Ju man, who, by casting lots, discovered what had happened, and told him that on her way back from the play Akim had crossed the river without making the customary sacrifice to the Water Ju Ju, and that, as the Ju Ju was angry, he had seized Akim and taken her to his home. He therefore told Akim's father to take one goat, one basketful of eggs, and one piece of white cloth to the river in the morning, and to offer them as a sacrifice to the Water Ju Ju; then Akim would be thrown out of the water seven times, but that if her father failed to catch her on the seventh time, she would disappear for ever.

Akim's father then returned home, and, when he arrived there, the little bird who had seen Akim taken by the Water Ju Ju, told him everything that had happened, confirming the Ju Ju's words. He also said that it was entirely the fault of the seven girls, who had refused to give Akim any food to make the sacrifice with.

Early the following morning the parents went to the river, and made the sacrifice as advised by the Ju Ju. Immediately they had done so, the Water Ju Ju threw Akim up from the middle of the river.[113] Her father caught her at once, and returned home very thankfully.

He never told anyone, however, that he had recovered his daughter, but made up his mind to punish the seven jealous girls, so he dug a deep pit in the middle of his house, and placed dried palm leaves and sharp stakes in the bottom of the pit. He then covered the top of the pit with new mats, and sent out word for all people to come and hold a play to rejoice with him, as he had recovered his daughter from the spirit land. Many people came, and danced and sang all the day and night, but the seven jealous girls did not appear, as they were frightened. However, as they were told that everything had gone well on the previous day, and that there had been no trouble, they went to the house the following morning and mixed with the dancers; but they were ashamed to look Akim in the face, who was sitting down in the middle of the dancing ring.

When Akim's father saw the seven girls he pretended to welcome them as his daughter's friends, and presented each of them with a brass rod, which he placed round their necks. He also gave them tombo to drink.

He then picked them out, and told them to go and sit on mats on the other side of the pit he had prepared for them. When they walked over the mats which hid the pit they all fell in, and Akim's father immediately got some red-hot ashes from the fire and threw them in on top of the screaming girls, who were in great pain. At once the dried palm leaves caught fire, killing all the girls at once.[114]

When the people heard the cries and saw the smoke, they all ran back to the town.

The next day the parents of the dead girls went to the head chief, and complained that Akim's father had killed their daughters, so the chief called him before him, and asked him for an explanation.

Akim's father went at once to the chief, taking the Ju Ju man, whom everybody relied upon, and the small bird, as his witnesses.

When the chief had heard the whole case, he told Akim's father that he should only have killed one girl to avenge his daughter, and not seven. So he told the father to bring Akim before him.

When she arrived, the head chief, seeing how beautiful she was, said that her father was justified in killing all the seven girls on her behalf, so he dismissed the case, and told the parents of the dead girls to go away and mourn for their daughters, who had been wicked and jealous women, and had been properly punished for their cruel behaviour to Akim.

72

MORAL.—Never kill a man or a woman because you are envious of their beauty, as if you do, you will surely be punished.

---

[115]

XXXI

How the Cannibals drove the People from Insofan Mountain to the Cross River (Ikom)

Very many years ago, before the oldest man alive at the present time can remember, the towns of Ikom, Okuni, Abijon, Insofan, Obokum, and all the other Injor towns were situated round and near the Insofan Mountain, and the head chief of the whole country was called Agbor. Abragba and Enfitop also lived there, and were also under King Agbor. The Insofan Mountain is about two days' march inland from the Cross River, and as none of the people there could swim, and knew nothing about canoes, they never went anywhere outside their own country, and were afraid to go down to the big river. The whole country was taken up with yam farms, and was divided amongst the various towns, each town having its own bush. At the end of each year, when it was time to dig the yams, there was a big play held, which was called the New Yam feast. At this festival there was always a big human sacrifice, fifty slaves being killed in one day. These slaves were tied up to trees in a row, and many drums were beaten; then a strong man, armed with a sharp matchet, went from one slave to another and cut their heads off. This was done to[116] cool the new yams, so that they would not hurt the stomachs of the people. Until this sacrifice was made no one in the country would eat a new yam, as they knew, if they did so, they would suffer great pain in their insides.

When the feast was held, all the towns brought one hundred yams each as a present to King Agbor. When the slaves were all killed fires were lit, and the dead bodies were placed over the fires to burn the hair off. A number of plantain leaves were then gathered and placed on the ground, and the bodies, having been cut into pieces, were placed on the plantain leaves.

When the yams were skinned, they were put into large pots, with water, oil, pepper, and salt. The cut-up bodies were then put in on top, and the pots covered up with other clay pots and left to boil for an hour.

73

The king, having called all the people together, then declared the New Yam feast had commenced, and singing and dancing were kept up for three days and nights, during which time much palm wine was consumed, and all the bodies and yams, which had been provided for them, were eaten by the people.

The heads were given to the king for his share, and, when he had finished eating them, the skulls were placed before the Ju Ju with some new yams, so that there should be a good crop the following season.

But although these natives ate the dead bodies of the slaves at the New Yam feast, they did not eat human flesh during the rest of the year.

This went on for many years, until at last the[117] Okuni people noticed that the graves of the people who had been buried were frequently dug open and the bodies removed. This caused great wonder, and, as they did not like the idea of their dead relations being taken away, they made a complaint to King Agbor. He at once caused a watch to be set on all newly dug graves, and that very night they caught seven men, who were very greedy, and used to come whenever a body was buried, dig it up, and carry it into the bush, where they made a fire, and cooked and ate it.

When they were caught, the people made them show where they lived, and where they cooked the bodies.

After walking for some hours in the forest, they came to a place where large heaps of human bones and skulls were found.

The seven men were then securely fastened up and brought before King Agbor, who held a large palaver of all the towns, and the whole situation was discussed.

Agbor said that this bad custom would necessitate all the towns separating, as they could not allow their dead relations to be dug up and eaten by these greedy people, and he could see no other way to prevent it. Agbor then gave one of the men to each of the seven towns, and told some of them to go on the far side of the big river and make their towns there. The others were to go farther down the river on the same side as Insofan Mountain, and when they found suitable places, they were each to kill their man as a sacrifice and then build their town.[118]

All the towns then departed, and when they had found good sites, they built their towns there.

When they had all gone, after a time Agbor began to feel very lonely, so he left the site of his old town and also went to the Cross River to live, so that he could see his friends.

After that the New Yam feast was held in each town, and the people still continued to kill and eat a few slaves at the feast, but the bodies of their relations and friends were kept for a long time above ground until they had become rotten, so that the greedy people should not dig them up and eat them.

This is why, even at the present time, the people do not like to bury their dead relations until they have become putrid.

[119]

XXXII

The Lucky Fisherman

In the olden days there were no hooks or casting nets, so that when the natives wanted to catch fish they made baskets and set traps at the river side.

One man named Akon Obo, who was very poor, began to make baskets and traps out of bamboo palm, and then when the river went down he used to take his traps to a pool and set them baited with palm-nuts. In the night the big fish used to smell the palm-nuts and go into the trap, when at once the door would fall down, and in the morning Akon Obo would go and take the fish out. He was very successful in his fishing, and used to sell the fish in the market for plenty of money. When he could afford to pay the dowry he married a woman named Eyong, a native of Okuni, and had three children by her, but he still continued his fishing. The eldest son was called Odey, the second Yambi, and the third Atuk. These three boys, when they grew up, helped their father with his fishing, and he gradually became wealthy and bought plenty of slaves. At last he joined the Egbo society, and became one of the chiefs of the town. Even after he became a chief, he and his sons still continued to fish.

One day, when he was crossing the river in a small dug-out canoe, a tornado came on very suddenly,[120] and the canoe capsized, drowning the chief. When his sons heard of the death of their father, they wanted to go and drown themselves also, but they were persuaded not to by the people. After searching for two days, they found the dead body some distance down the river, and brought it back to the town. They then called their company together to play, dance, and sing for twelve days, in accordance with their native custom, and much palm wine was drunk.

When the play was finished, they took their father's body to a hollowed-out cavern, and placed two live slaves with it, one holding a native lamp of palm-oil, and the other holding a matchet. They were both tied up, so that they could not escape, and were left there to keep watch over the dead chief, until they died of starvation.

When the cave was covered in, the sons called the chiefs together, and they played Egbo[9] for seven days, which used up a lot of their late father's money. When the play was over, the chiefs were surprised at the amount of money which the sons had been able to spend on the funeral of their father, as they knew how poor he had been as a young man. They therefore called him the lucky fisherman.

FOOTNOTES

[9]The Egbo society would meet together and would be provided with palm wine and food, as much as they could eat and drink, which frequently cost a lot of money. Dancing and singing would also be kept up and a band would play, consisting of drums made of hollowed-out trunks of trees, beaten with two pieces of soft wood, native made bells and rattles made of basket work, with stones inside, the bottom consisting of hard dried skin, and covered all over with long streamers of fibre. Other drums are also played by hand; these are made out of hollow wood, covered at one end with dried skin, the other end being left open. The drummer usually sits on two of these drums, which have a different note, one being a deep sound, and the other slightly higher.

[121]

XXXIII

The Orphan Boy and the Magic Stone

A chief of Inde named Inkita had a son named Ayong Kita, whose mother had died at his birth.

The old chief was a hunter, and used to take his son out with him when he went into the bush. He used to do most of his hunting in the long grass which grows over nearly all the Inde country, and used to kill plenty of bush buck in the dry season.

In those days the people had no guns, so the chief had to shoot everything he got with his bow and arrows, which required a lot of skill.

When his little son was old enough, he gave him a small bow and some small arrows, and taught him how to shoot. The little boy was very quick at learning, and by continually practising at lizards and small birds, soon became expert in the use of his little bow, and could hit them almost every time he shot at them.

When the boy was ten years old his father died, and as he thus became the head of his father's house, and was in authority over all the slaves, they became very discontented, and made plans to kill him, so he ran away into the bush.

Having nothing to eat, he lived for several days on the nuts which fell from the palm trees. He[122] was too young to kill any large animals, and only had his small bow and arrows, with which he killed a few squirrels, bush rats, and small birds, and so managed to live.

Now once at night, when he was sleeping in the hollow of a tree, he had a dream in which his father appeared, and told him where there was plenty of treasure buried in the earth, but, being a small boy, he was frightened, and did not go to the place.

One day, some time after the dream, having walked far and being very thirsty, he went to a lake, and was just going to drink, when he heard a hissing sound, and heard a voice tell him not to drink. Not seeing any one, he was afraid, and ran away without drinking.

Early next morning, when he was out with his bow trying to shoot some small animal, he met an old woman with quite long hair. She was so ugly that he thought she must be a witch, so he tried to run, but she told him not to fear, as she wanted to help him and assist him to rule over his late father's house. She also told him that it was she who had called out to him at the lake not to drink, as there was a bad Ju Ju in the water which would have killed him. The old woman then took Ayong to a stream some little distance from the lake, and bending down, took out a small shining stone from the water, which she gave to him, at the same time telling him to go to the place which his father had advised him to visit in his dream. She then said, "When you get there you must dig, and you will find plenty of money; you must then go and buy two strong slaves, and when you have got them, you[123] must take them into the forest, away from the town, and get them to build you a house with several rooms in it. You must then place the stone in one of the rooms, and whenever you want anything, all you have to do is to go into the room and tell the stone what you want, and your wishes will be at once gratified."

Ayong did as the old woman told him, and after much difficulty and danger bought the two slaves and built a house in the forest, taking great care of the precious stone, which he placed in an inside room. Then for some time, whenever he wanted anything, he used to go into the room and ask for a sufficient number of rods to buy what he wanted, and they were always brought at once.

This went on for many years, and Ayong grew up to be a man, and became very rich, and bought many slaves, having made friends with the Aro men, who in those days used to do a big traffic in slaves. After ten years had passed Ayong had quite a large town and many slaves, but one night the old woman appeared to him in a dream and told him that she thought that he was sufficiently wealthy, and that it was time for him to return the magic stone to the small stream from whence it came. But Ayong, although he was rich, wanted to rule his father's house and be a head chief for all the Inde country, so he sent for all the Ju Ju men in the country and two witch men, and marched with all his slaves to his father's town. Before he started he held a big palaver, and told them to point out any slave who had a bad heart, and who might kill him when he came to rule the country. Then the Ju Ju men[124] consulted together, and pointed out fifty of the slaves who, they said, were witches, and would try to kill Ayong. He at once had them made prisoners, and tried them by the ordeal of Esere bean[10] to see whether they were witches or not. As none of them could vomit the beans they all died, and were declared to be witches. He then had them buried at once. When the remainder of his slaves saw what had happened, they all came to him and begged his pardon, and promised to serve him faithfully. Although the fifty men were buried they could not rest, and troubled Ayong very much, and after a time he became very sick himself, so he sent again for the Ju Ju men, who told him that it was the witch men who, although they were dead and buried, had power to come out at night and used to suck Ayong's blood, which was the cause of his sickness. They then said, "We are only three Ju Ju men; you must get seven more of us, making the magic number of ten." When they came they dug up the bodies of the fifty witches, and found they were quite fresh. Then Ayong had big fires made, and burned them one after the other, and gave the Ju Ju men a big present. He soon after became quite well again, and took possession of his father's property, and ruled over all the country.

[125]

Ever since then, whenever anyone is accused of being a witch, they are tried by the ordeal of the poisonous Esere bean, and if they can vomit they do not die, and are declared innocent, but if they cannot do so, they die in great pain.

FOOTNOTES

[10] The Esere or Calabar bean is a strong poison, and was formerly much used by the natives. These beans are ground up in a stone mortar, and are then swallowed by the accused person. If the man dies he is considered guilty, but if he lives, he is supposed to have proved his innocence of whatever the charge may have been which was brought against him. Death generally ensues

about two hours after the poison is administered. If the accused takes a sufficient amount of the ground-up beans to make him vomit it will probably save his life, otherwise he will die in great pain.

[126]

XXXIV

The Slave Girl who tried to Kill her Mistress

A man called Akpan, who was a native of Oku, a town in the Ibibio country, admired a girl called Emme very much, who lived at Ibibio, and wished to marry her, as she was the finest girl in her company. It was the custom in those days for the parents to demand such a large amount for their daughters as dowry, that if after they were married they failed to get on with their husbands, as they could not redeem themselves, they were sold as slaves. Akpan paid a very large sum as dowry for Emme, and she was put in the fatting-house until the proper time arrived for her to marry.

Akpan told the parents that when their daughter was ready they must send her over to him. This they promised to do. Emme's father was a rich man, and after seven years had elapsed, and it became time for her to go to her husband, he saw a very fine girl, who had also just come out of the fatting-house, and whom the parents wished to sell as a slave. Emme's father therefore bought her, and gave her to his daughter as her handmaiden.

The next day Emme's little sister, being very anxious to go with her, obtained the consent of her mother, and they started off together, the slave girl[127] carrying a large bundle containing clothes and presents from Emme's father. Akpan's house was a long day's march from where they lived. When they arrived just outside the town they came to a spring, where the people used to get their drinking water from, but no one was allowed to bathe there. Emme, however, knew nothing about this. They took off their clothes to wash close to the spring, and where there was a deep hole which led to the Water Ju Ju's house. The slave girl knew of this Ju Ju, and thought if she could get her mistress to bathe, she would be taken by the Ju Ju, and she would then be able to take her place and marry Akpan. So they went down to bathe, and when they were close to the water the slave girl pushed her mistress in, and she at once disappeared. The little girl then began to cry, but the slave girl said, "If you cry any more I will kill

79

you at once, and throw your body into the hole after your sister." And she told the child that she must never mention what had happened to any one, and particularly not to Akpan, as she was going to represent her sister and marry him, and that if she ever told any one what she had seen, she would be killed at once. She then made the little girl carry her load to Akpan's house.

When they arrived, Akpan was very much disappointed at the slave girl's appearance, as she was not nearly as pretty and fine as he had expected her to be; but as he had not seen Emme for seven years, he had no suspicion that the girl was not really Emme, for whom he had paid such a large dowry. He then called all his company together to play and feast, and when they arrived they were[128] much astonished, and said, "Is this the fine woman for whom you paid so much dowry, and whom you told us so much about?" And Akpan could not answer them.

The slave girl was then for some time very cruel to Emme's little sister, and wanted her to die, so that her position would be more secure with her husband. She beat the little girl every day, and always made her carry the largest water-pot to the spring; she also made the child place her finger in the fire to use as firewood. When the time came for food, the slave girl went to the fire and got a burning piece of wood and burned the child all over the body with it. When Akpan asked her why she treated the child so badly, she replied that she was a slave that her father had bought for her. When the little girl took the heavy water-pot to the river to fill it there was no one to lift it up for her, so that she could not get it on to her head; she therefore had to remain a long time at the spring, and at last began calling for her sister Emme to come and help her.

When Emme heard her little sister crying for her, she begged the Water Ju Ju to allow her to go and help her, so he told her she might go, but that she must return to him again immediately. When the little girl saw her sister she did not want to leave her, and asked to be allowed to go into the hole with her. She then told Emme how very badly she had been treated by the slave girl, and her elder sister told her to have patience and wait, that a day of vengeance would arrive sooner or later. The little girl went back to Akpan's house with a glad heart as she had seen her sister, but when she got to the[129] house, the slave girl said, "Why have you been so long getting the water?" and then took another stick from the fire and burnt the little girl again very badly, and starved her for the rest of the day.

This went on for some time, until, one day, when the child went to the river for water, after all the people had gone, she cried out for her sister as usual, but she did not come for a long time, as there was a hunter from Akpan's town hidden near watching the hole, and the Water Ju Ju told Emme that she must not go; but, as the little girl went on crying bitterly, Emme at last persuaded the Ju Ju to let her go, promising to return quickly. When she emerged from the water, she looked very beautiful with the rays of the setting sun shining on her glistening body. She helped her little sister with her water-pot, and then disappeared into the hole again.

The hunter was amazed at what he had seen, and when he returned, he told Akpan what a beautiful woman had come out of the water and had helped the little girl with her water-pot. He also told Akpan that he was convinced that the girl he had seen at the spring was his proper wife, Emme, and that the Water Ju Ju must have taken her.

Akpan then made up his mind to go out and watch and see what happened, so, in the early morning the hunter came for him, and they both went down to the river, and hid in the forest near the water-hole.

When Akpan saw Emme come out of the water, he recognised her at once, and went home and considered how he should get her out of the power[130] of the Water Ju Ju. He was advised by some of his friends to go to an old woman, who frequently made sacrifices to the Water Ju Ju, and consult her as to what was the best thing to do.

When he went to her, she told him to bring her one white slave, one white goat, one piece of white cloth, one white chicken, and a basket of eggs. Then, when the great Ju Ju day arrived, she would take them to the Water Ju Ju, and make a sacrifice of them on his behalf. The day after the sacrifice was made, the Water Ju Ju would return the girl to her, and she would bring her to Akpan.

Akpan then bought the slave, and took all the other things to the old woman, and, when the day of the sacrifice arrived, he went with his friend the hunter and witnessed the old woman make the sacrifice. The slave was bound up and led to the hole, then the old woman called to the Water Ju Ju and cut the slave's throat with a sharp knife and pushed him into the hole. She then did the same to the goat and chicken, and also threw the eggs and cloth in on top of them.

After this had been done, they all returned to their homes. The next morning at dawn the old woman went to the hole, and found Emme standing at the side of the spring, so she told her that she was her friend, and was going to take her to her husband. She then took Emme back to her own home, and hid her in her room, and sent word to Akpan to come to her house, and to take great care that the slave woman knew nothing about the matter.

So Akpan left the house secretly by the back door,[131] and arrived at the old woman's house without meeting anybody.

When Emme saw Akpan, she asked for her little sister, so he sent his friend, the hunter, for her to the spring, and he met her carrying her water-pot to get the morning supply of water for the house, and brought her to the old woman's house with him.

When Emme had embraced her sister, she told her to return to the house and do something to annoy the slave woman, and then she was to run as fast as she could back to the old woman's house, where, no doubt, the slave girl would follow her, and would meet them all inside the house, and see Emme, who she believed she had killed.

The little girl did as she was told, and, directly she got into the house, she called out to the slave woman: "Do you know that you are a wicked woman, and have treated me very badly? I know you are only my sister's slave, and you will be properly punished." She then ran as hard as she could to the old woman's house. Directly the slave woman heard what the little girl said, she was quite mad with rage, and seized a burning stick from the fire, and ran after the child; but the little one got to the house first, and ran inside, the slave woman following close upon her heels with the burning stick in her hand.

Then Emme came out and confronted the slave woman, and she at once recognised her mistress, whom she thought she had killed, so she stood quite still.

Then they all went back to Akpan's house, and[132] when they arrived there, Akpan asked the slave woman what she meant by pretending that she was Emme, and why she had tried to kill her. But, seeing she was found out, the slave woman had nothing to say.

Many people were then called to a play to celebrate the recovery of Akpan's wife, and when they had all come, he told them what the slave woman had done.

After this, Emme treated the slave girl in the same way as she had treated her little sister. She made her put her fingers in the fire, and burnt her with sticks. She also made her beat foo-foo with her head in a hollowed-out tree, and after a time she was tied up to a tree and starved to death.

Ever since that time, when a man marries a girl, he is always present when she comes out of the fatting-house and takes her home himself, so that such evil things as happened to Emme and her sister may not occur again.

[133]

AFRICAN SCHOLAR PUBLICATIONS
www.lulu.com/egipt

XXXV

The King and the 'Nsiat Bird

When 'Ndarake was King of Idu, being young and rich, he was very fond of fine girls, and had plenty of slaves. The 'Nsiat bird was then living at Idu, and had a very pretty daughter, whom 'Ndarake wished to marry. When he spoke to the father about the matter, he replied that of course he had no objection personally, as it would be a great honour for his daughter to marry the king, but, unfortunately, when any of his family had children, they always gave birth to twins, which, as the king knew, was not allowed in the country; the native custom being to kill both the children and throw them into the bush, the mother being driven away and allowed to starve. The king, however, being greatly struck with Adit, the bird's daughter, insisted on marrying her, so the 'Nsiat bird had to agree. A large amount of dowry was paid by the king, and a big play and feast was held. One strong slave was told to carry Adit 'Nsiat during the whole play, and she sat on his shoulders with her legs around his neck; this was done to show what a rich and powerful man the king was.

After the marriage, in due course Adit gave birth to twins, as her mother had done before her. The[134] king immediately became very fond of the two babies, but according to the native custom, which was too strong for any one to resist, he had to give them up to be killed. When the 'Nsiat bird heard this, he went to the king and reminded him that he had warned the king before he married what would happen if he married Adit, and rather than that the twins should be killed, he and the whole of his family would leave the earth and dwell in the air, taking the twins with them. As the king was so fond of Adit and the two children, and did not want them to be killed, he gladly consented, and the 'Nsiat bird took the whole of his family, as well as Adit and her two children, away, and left the earth to live and make their home in the trees; but as they had formerly lived in the town with all the people, they did not like to go into the forest, so they made their nests in the trees which grew in the town, and that is why you always see the 'Nsiat birds living and making their nests only in places where human beings are. The black birds are the cocks, and the golden-coloured ones are the hens. It was the beautiful colour of Adit which first attracted the attention of 'Ndarake and caused him to marry her.

---

[135]

XXXVI

Concerning the Fate of Essido and his Evil Companions

Chief Oborri lived at a town called Adiagor, which is on the right bank of the Calabar River. He was a wealthy chief, and belonged to the Egbo Society. He had many large canoes, and plenty of slaves to paddle them. These canoes he used to fill up with new yams—each canoe being under one head slave and containing eight paddles; the canoes were capable of holding three puncheons of palm-oil, and cost eight hundred rods each. When they were full, about ten of them used to start off together and paddle to Rio del Rey. They went through creeks all the way, which run through mangrove swamps, with palm-oil trees here and there. Sometimes in the tornado season it was very dangerous crossing the creeks, as the canoes were so heavily laden, having only a few inches above the water, that quite a small wave would fill the canoe and cause it to sink to the bottom. Although most of the boys could swim, it often happened that some of them were lost, as there are many large alligators in these waters. After four days' hard paddling they would arrive at Rio del Rey, where they had very little[136] difficulty in exchanging their new yams for bags of dried shrimps and sticks with smoked fish on them.[11]

Chief Oborri had two sons, named Eyo I. and Essido. Their mother having died when they were babies, the children were brought up by their father. As they grew up, they developed entirely different characters. The eldest was very hard-working and led a solitary life; but the younger son was fond of gaiety and was very lazy, in fact, he spent most of his time in the neighbouring towns playing and dancing. When the two boys arrived at the respective ages of eighteen and twenty their father died, and they were left to look after themselves. According to native custom, the elder son, Eyo I., was entitled to the whole of his father's estate; but being very fond of his younger brother, he gave him a large number of rods and some land with a house. Immediately Essido became possessed of the money he became wilder than ever, gave big feasts to his companions, and always had his house full of women, upon whom he spent large sums. Although the amount his brother had given him on his father's death was very large, in the course of a few years [137]Essido had spent it all. He then sold his house and effects, and spent the proceeds on feasting.

While he had been living this gay and unprofitable life, Eyo I. had been working harder than ever at his father's old trade, and had made many trips to Rio del Rey himself. Almost every week he had canoes laden with yams going down river and returning after about twelve days with shrimps and fish, which Eyo I. himself disposed of in the neighbouring markets, and he very rapidly became a rich man. At intervals he remonstrated with Essido on his extravagance, but his warnings had no effect; if anything, his brother became worse. At last the time arrived when all his money was spent, so Essido went to his brother and asked him to lend him two thousand rods, but Eyo refused, and told Essido that he would not help him in any way to continue his present life of debauchery, but that if he liked to work on the farm and trade, he would give him a fair share of the profits. This Essido indignantly refused, and went back to the town and consulted some of the very few friends he had left as to what was the best thing to do.

The men he spoke to were thoroughly bad men, and had been living upon Essido for a long time. They suggested to him that he should go round the town and borrow money from the people he had entertained, and then they would run away to Akpabryos town, which was about four days' march from Calabar. This Essido did, and managed to borrow a lot of money, although many people refused to lend him anything. Then at night he set off with his evil companions, who carried his money, as they had not been able to borrow any themselves,[138] being so well known. When they arrived at Akpabryos town they found many beautiful women and graceful dancers. They then started the same life again, until after a few weeks most of the money had gone. They then met and consulted together how to get more money, and advised Essido to return to his rich brother, pretending that he was going to work and give up his old life; he should then get poison from a man they knew of, and place it in his brother's food, so that he would die, and then Essido would become possessed of all his brother's wealth, and they would be able to live in the same way as they had formerly. Essido, who had sunk very low, agreed to this plan, and they left Akpabryos town the next morning. After marching for two days, they arrived at a small hut in the bush where a man who was an expert poisoner lived, called Okponesip. He was the head Ju Ju man of the country, and when they had bribed him with eight hundred rods he swore them to secrecy, and gave Essido a small parcel containing a deadly poison which he said would kill his brother in three months. All he had to do was to place the poison in his brother's food.

When Essido returned to his brother's house he pretended to be very sorry for his former mode of living, and said that for the future he was going to work. Eyo I. was very glad when he heard this, and at once asked his brother in, and gave him new clothes and plenty to eat.

In the evening, when supper was being prepared, Essido went into the kitchen, pretending he wanted to get a light from the fire for his pipe. The cook[139] being absent and no one about, he put the poison in the soup, and then returned to the living-room. He then asked for some tombo, which was brought, and when he had finished it, he said he did not want any supper, and went to sleep. His brother, Eyo I., had supper by himself and consumed all the soup. In a week's time he began to feel very ill, and as the days passed he became worse, so he sent for his Ju Ju man.

When Essido saw him coming, he quietly left the house; but the Ju Ju man, by casting lots, very soon discovered that it was Essido who had given poison to his brother. When he told Eyo I. this, he would not believe it, and sent him away. However, when Essido returned, his elder brother told him what the Ju Ju man had said, but that he did not believe him for one moment, and had sent him away. Essido was much relieved when he heard this, but as he was anxious that no suspicion of the crime should be attached to him, he went to the Household Ju Ju,[12] and having first sworn that he had never administered poison to his brother, he drank out of the pot.

Three months after he had taken the poison [140]Eyo I. died, much to the grief of everyone who knew him, as he was much respected, not only on account of his great wealth, but because he was also an upright and honest man, who never did harm to anyone.

Essido kept his brother's funeral according to the usual custom, and there was much playing and dancing, which was kept up for a long time. Then Essido paid off his old creditors in order to make himself popular, and kept open house, entertaining most lavishly, and spending his money in many foolish ways. All the bad women about collected at his house, and his old evil companions went on as they had done before.

Things got so bad that none of the respectable people would have anything to do with him, and at last the chiefs of the country, seeing the way Essido was squandering his late brother's estate, assembled together, and eventually came to the conclusion that he was a witch man, and had poisoned his brother in order to acquire his position. The chiefs, who were all friends of the late Eyo, and who were very sorry at the death, as they knew that if he had lived he would have become a great and powerful chief, made up their minds to give Essido the Ekpawor Ju Ju, which is a very strong medicine, and gets into men's heads, so that when they have drunk it they are compelled to speak the truth, and if they have done wrong they die very shortly. Essido was then told to dress himself and attend the meeting at the palaver house, and when he arrived the chiefs charged him with having killed his brother by witchcraft. Essido[141] denied having done so, but the chiefs told him that if he were innocent he must prove it by drinking the bowl of Ekpawor medicine which was placed before him. As he could not refuse to drink, he drank the bowl off in great fear and trembling, and very soon the Ju Ju having got hold of him, he confessed that he had poisoned his brother, but that his friends had advised him to do so. About two hours after drinking the Ekpawor, Essido died in great pain.

The friends were then brought to the meeting and tied up to posts, and questioned as to the part they had taken in the death of Eyo. As they were too frightened to answer, the chiefs told them that they knew from Essido that they had induced him to poison his brother. They were then taken to the place where Eyo was buried, the grave having been dug open, and their heads were cut off and fell into the grave, and their bodies were thrown in after them as a sacrifice for the wrong they had done. The grave was then filled up again.

Ever since that time, whenever anyone is suspected of being a witch, he is tried by the Ekpawor Ju Ju.

FOOTNOTES

[11]A stick of fish consisted of two sticks with a big fish in the middle of each and small fish at each end, there being eight fish on each stick, making sixteen in all. These sticks were then tied together, and smoked over wood fires until they were quite dried. One stick of fish would sell at Calabar in the dry season time for from 3s. 6d. to 5s. a stick, and a stick would be got for five large yams which cost Chief Oborri only 1s., so a large profit was made on each canoe load—the canoes carrying about a thousand yams each. A bag of shrimps would be bartered for twenty-five large yams, and the shrimps would be sold for 15s., being a profit of 10s. on each bag. At the present time, however, the same sized bag of shrimps, in the wet season, would sell at Calabar for £3, 10s., and in the dry season for between £1, 10s. and £2.

[12]Every compound has a small Ju Ju in the centre, which generally consists of a few curiously shaped stones and a small tree on which the 'Nsiat bird frequently builds. There is sometimes a species of cactus at the foot, an earthenware pot is supported on sticks against the tree, and tied on with tie-tie, or native rope. In this pot there is always a very foul-smelling liquid, with frequently some rotten eggs floating in it. Small sacrifices are made to these Ju Ju's of chickens, &c., and this Ju Ju is frequently appealed to. The liquid is sometimes taken as a specific against sickness or poison. In the dry season the author has often observed large spiders with their webs all over these Ju Ju's, but they are never touched. There is also frequently a roughly carved image of wood, and sometimes an old matchet and some broken earthenware on the ground, with a brass rod or manilla. It is generally a very dirty spot.

[142]

XXXVII

Concerning the Hawk and the Owl

In the olden days when Effiong was king of Calabar, it was customary at that time for rulers to give big feasts, to which all the subjects and all the birds of the air and animals of the forest, also the fish and other things that lived in the water, were invited. All the people, birds, animals, and fish, were under the king, and had to obey him. His favourite messenger was the hawk, as he could travel so quickly.

The hawk served the king faithfully for several years, and when he wanted to retire, he asked what the king proposed to do for him, as very soon he would be too old to work any more. So the king told the hawk to bring any living creature, bird or animal, to him, and he would allow the hawk for the future to live on that particular species without any trouble. The hawk then flew over a lot of country, and went from forest to forest, until at last he found a young owl which had tumbled out of its nest. This the hawk brought to the king, who told him that for the future he might eat owls. The hawk then carried the owlet away, and told his friends what the king had said.

One of the wisest of them said, "Tell me when[143] you seized the young owlet, what did the parents say?" And the hawk replied that the father and mother owls kept quite quiet, and never said anything. The hawk's friend then advised him to return the owlet to his parents, as he could never tell what the owls would do to him in the night-time, and as they had made no noise, they were no doubt plotting in their minds some deep and cruel revenge.

The next day the hawk carried the owlet back to his parents and left him near the nest. He then flew about, trying to find some other bird which would do as his food; but as all the birds had heard that the hawk had seized the owlet, they hid themselves, and would not come out when the hawk was near. He therefore could not catch any birds.

As he was flying home he saw a lot of fowls near a house, basking in the sun and scratching in the dust. There were also several small chickens running about and chasing insects, or picking up anything they could find to eat, with the old hen following them and clucking and calling to them from time to time. When the hawk saw the chickens, he made up his mind that he would take one, so he swooped down and caught the smallest in his strong claws. Immediately he had seized the chicken the cocks began to make a great noise, and the hen ran after him and tried to make him drop her child, calling loudly, with her feathers fluffed out and making dashes at him. But he carried it off, and all the fowls and chickens at once ran screaming into the houses, some taking shelter under bushes and others trying to hide themselves[144] in the long grass. He then carried the chicken to the king, telling him that he had returned the owlet to his parents, as he did not want him for food; so the king told the hawk that for the future he could always feed on chickens.

The hawk then took the chicken home, and his friend who dropped in to see him, asked him what the parents of the chicken had done when they saw their child taken away; so the hawk said—

"They all made a lot of noise, and the old hen chased me, but although there was a great disturbance amongst the fowls, nothing happened."

His friend then said as the fowls had made much palaver, he was quite safe to kill and eat the chickens, as the people who made plenty of noise in the daytime would go to sleep at night and not disturb him, or do him any injury; the only people to be afraid of were those who when they were injured, kept quite silent; you might be certain then that they were plotting mischief, and would do harm in the night-time.

---

[145]

XXXVIII

The Story of the Drummer and the Alligators

There was once a woman named Affiong Any who lived at 'Nsidung, a small town to the south of Calabar. She was married to a chief of Hensham Town called Etim Ekeng. They had lived together for several years, but had no children. The chief was very anxious to have a child during his lifetime, and made sacrifices to his Ju Ju, but they had no effect. So he went to a witch man, who told him that the reason he had no children was that he was too rich. The chief then asked the witch man how he should spend his money in order to get a child, and he was told to make friends with everybody, and give big feasts, so that he should get rid of some of his money and become poorer.

The chief then went home and told his wife. The next day his wife called all her company together and gave them a big dinner, which cost a lot of money; much food was consumed, and large quantities of tombo were drunk. Then the chief entertained his company, which cost a lot more money. He also wasted a lot of money in the Egbo house. When half of his property was wasted, his wife told him that she had conceived. The chief, being very glad, called a big play for the next day.[146]

In those days all the rich chiefs of the country belonged to the Alligator Company, and used to meet in the water. The reason they belonged to the company was, first of all, to protect their canoes when they went trading, and secondly, to destroy the canoes and property of the people who did not belong to their company, and to take their money and kill their slaves.

Chief Etim Ekeng was a kind man, and would not join this society, although he was repeatedly urged to do so. After a time a son was born to the chief, and he called him Edet Etim. The chief then called the Egbo society together, and all the doors of the houses in the town were shut, the markets were stopped, and the women were not allowed to go outside their houses while the Egbo was playing. This was kept up for several days, and cost the chief a lot of money. Then he made up his mind that he would divide his property, and give his son half when he became old enough. Unfortunately after three months the chief died, leaving his sorrowing wife to look after their little child.

The wife then went into mourning for seven years for her husband, and after that time she became entitled to all his property, as the late chief had no brothers. She looked after the little boy very carefully until he grew up, when he became a very fine, healthy young man, and was much admired by all the pretty girls of the town; but his mother warned him strongly not to go with them, because they would make him become a bad man. Whenever the girls had a play they used to invite Edet Etim, and at last he went to the play, and they made him beat the[147] drum for them to dance to. After much practice he became the best drummer in the town, and whenever the girls had a play they always called him to drum for them. Plenty of the young girls left their husbands, and went to Edet and asked him to marry them. This made all the young men of the town very jealous, and when they met together at night they considered what would be the best way to kill him. At last they decided that when Edet went to bathe they would induce the alligators to take him. So one night, when he was washing, one alligator seized him by the foot, and others came and seized him round the waist. He fought very hard, but at last they dragged him into the deep water, and took him to their home.

When his mother heard this, she determined to do her best to recover her son, so she kept quite quiet until the morning.

When the young men saw that Edet's mother remained quiet, and did not cry, they thought of the story of the hawk and the owl, and determined to keep Edet alive for a few months.

90

At cockcrow the mother raised a cry, and went to the grave of her dead husband in order to consult his spirit as to what she had better do to recover her lost son. After a time she went down to the beach with small young green branches in her hands, with which she beat the water, and called upon all the Ju Jus of the Calabar River to help her to recover her son. She then went home and got a load of rods, and took them to a Ju Ju man in the farm. His name was Ininen Okon; he was so called because he was very artful, and had plenty of strong Ju Jus.[148]

When the young boys heard that Edet's mother had gone to Ininen Okon, they all trembled with fear, and wanted to return Edet, but they could not do so, as it was against the rules of their society. The Ju Ju man having discovered that Edet was still alive, and was being detained in the alligators' house, told the mother to be patient. After three days Ininen himself joined another alligators' society, and went to inspect the young alligators' house. He found a young man whom he knew, left on guard when all the alligators had gone to feed at the ebb of the tide, and came back and told the mother to wait, as he would make a Ju Ju which would cause them all to depart in seven days, and leave no one in the house. He made his Ju Ju, and the young alligators said that, as no one had come for Edet, they would all go at the ebb tide to feed, and leave no one in charge of the house. When they returned they found Edet still there, and everything as they had left it, as Ininen had not gone that day.

Three days afterwards they all went away again, and this time went a long way off, and did not return quickly. When Ininen saw that the tide was going down he changed himself into an alligator, and swam to the young alligators' home, where he found Edet chained to a post. He then found an axe and cut the post, releasing the boy. But Edet, having been in the water so long, was deaf and dumb. He then found several loin cloths which had been left behind by the young alligators, so he gathered them together and took them away to show to the king, and Ininen left the place, taking Edet with him.[149]

He then called the mother to see her son, but when she came the boy could only look at her, and could not speak. The mother embraced her boy, but he took no notice, as he did not seem capable of understanding anything, but sat down quietly. Then the Ju Ju man told Edet's mother that he would cure her son in a few days, so he made several Ju Jus, and gave her son medicine, and after a time the boy recovered his speech and became sensible again.

Then Edet's mother put on a mourning cloth, and pretended that her son was dead, and did not tell the people he had come back to her. When the young alligators returned, they found that Edet was gone, and that some one had taken their loin cloths. They were therefore much afraid, and made inquiries if Edet had been seen, but they could hear nothing about him, as he was hidden in a farm, and the mother continued to wear her mourning cloth in order to deceive them.

Nothing happened for six months, and they had quite forgotten all about the matter. Affiong, the mother, then went to the chiefs of the town, and asked them to hold a large meeting of all the people, both young and old, at the palaver house, so that her late husband's property might be divided up in accordance with the native custom, as her son had been killed by the alligators.

The next day the chiefs called all the people together, but the mother in the early morning took her son to a small room at the back of the palaver house, and left him there with the seven loin cloths which the Ju Ju man had taken from the alligators' home.[150] When the chiefs and all the people were seated, Affiong stood up and addressed them, saying—

"Chiefs and young men of my town, eight years ago my husband was a fine young man. He married me, and we lived together for many years without having any children. At last I had a son, but my husband died a few months afterwards. I brought my boy up carefully, but as he was a good drummer and dancer the young men were jealous, and had him caught by the alligators. Is there any one present who can tell me what my son would have become if he had lived?" She then asked them what they thought of the alligator society, which had killed so many young men.

The chiefs, who had lost a lot of slaves, told her that if she could produce evidence against any members of the society they would destroy it at once. She then called upon Ininen to appear with her son Edet. He came out from the room leading Edet by the hand, and placed the bundle of loin cloths before the chiefs.

The young men were very much surprised when they saw Edet, and wanted to leave the palaver house; but when they stood up to go the chiefs told them to sit down at once, or they would receive three hundred lashes. They then sat down, and the Ju Ju man explained how he had gone to the alligators' home, and had brought Edet back to his mother. He also said that he had found the seven loin cloths in the house, but he did not wish to say anything about them, as the owners of some of the cloths were sons of the chiefs.

The chiefs, who were anxious to stop the bad [151] society, told him, however, to speak at once and tell them everything. Then he undid the bundle and took the cloths out one by one, at the same time calling upon the owners to come and take them. When they came to take their cloths, they were told to remain where they were; and they were then told to name their company. The seven young men then gave the names of all the members of their society, thirty-two in all. These men were all placed in a line, and the chiefs then passed sentence, which was that they should all be killed the next morning on the beach. So they were then all tied together to posts, and seven men were placed as a guard over them. They made fires and beat drums all the night.

Early in the morning, at about 4 A.M., the big wooden drum was placed on the roof of the palaver house, and beaten to celebrate the death of the evildoers, which was the custom in those days.

The boys were then unfastened from the posts, and had their hands tied behind their backs, and were marched down to the beach. When they arrived there, the head chief stood up and addressed the people. "This is a small town of which I am chief, and I am determined to stop this bad custom, as so many men have been killed." He then told a man who had a sharp matchet to cut off one man's head. He then told another man who had a sharp knife to skin another young man alive. A third man who had a heavy stick was ordered to beat another to death, and so the chief went on and killed all the thirty-two young men in the most[152] horrible ways he could think of. Some of them were tied to posts in the river, and left there until the tide came up and drowned them. Others were flogged to death.

After they had all been killed, for many years no one was killed by alligators, but some little time afterwards on the road between the beach and the town the land fell in, making a very large and deep hole, which was said to be the home of the alligators, and the people have ever since tried to fill it up, but have never yet been able to do so.

---

[153]

XXXIX

The 'Nsasak Bird and the Odudu Bird

A long time ago, in the days of King Adam of Calabar, the king wanted to know if there was any animal or bird which was capable of enduring hunger for a long period. When he found one the king said he would make him a chief of his tribe.

The 'Nsasak bird is very small, having a shining breast of green and red; he also has blue and yellow feathers and red round the neck, and his chief food consists of ripe palm nuts. The Odudu bird, on the other hand, is much larger, about the size of a magpie, with plenty of feathers, but a very thin body; he has a long tail, and his colouring is black and brown with a cream-coloured breast. He lives chiefly on grasshoppers, and is also very fond of crickets, which make a noise at night.

Both the 'Nsasak bird and the Odudu were great friends, and used to live together. They both made up their minds that they would go before the king and try to be made chiefs, but the Odudu bird was quite confident that he would win, as he was so much bigger than the 'Nsasak bird. He therefore offered to starve for seven days.

The king then told them both to build houses which he would inspect, and then he would have[154] them fastened up, and the one who could remain the longest without eating would be made the chief.

They both then built their houses, but the 'Nsasak bird, who was very cunning, thought that he could not possibly live for seven days without eating anything. He therefore made a tiny hole in the wall (being very small himself), which he covered up so that the king would not notice it on his inspection. The king then came and looked carefully over both houses, but failed to detect the little hole in the 'Nsasak bird's house, as it had been hidden so carefully. He therefore declared that both houses were safe, and then ordered the two birds to go inside their respective houses, and the doors were carefully fastened on the outside.

Every morning at dawn the 'Nsasak bird used to escape through the small opening he had left high up in the wall, and fly away a long distance and enjoy himself all day, taking care, however, that none of the people on the farms should see him. Then when the sun went down he would fly back to his little house and creep through the hole in the wall, closing it carefully after him. When he was safely inside he would call out to his friend the Odudu and ask him if he felt hungry, and told him that he must bear it well if he wanted to win, as he, the 'Nsasak bird, was very fit, and could go on for a long time.

For several days this went on, the voice of the Odudu bird growing weaker and weaker every night, until at last he could no longer reply. Then the little bird knew that his friend must be dead. He was very sorry, but could not report the matter, as he was supposed to be confined inside his house.[155]

When the seven days had expired the king came and had both the doors of the houses opened. The 'Nsasak bird at once flew out, and, perching on a branch of a tree which grew near, sang most merrily; but the Odudu bird was found to be quite dead, and there was very little left of him, as the ants had eaten most of his body, leaving only the feathers and bones on the floor.

The king therefore at once appointed the 'Nsasak bird to be the head chief of all the small birds, and in the Ibibio country even to the present time the small boys who have bows and arrows are presented with a prize, which sometimes takes the shape of a female goat, if they manage to shoot a 'Nsasak bird, as the 'Nsasak bird is the king of the small birds, and most difficult to shoot on account of his wiliness and his small size.

---

[156]

XL

The Election of the King Bird (the black-and-white Fishing Eagle)

Old Town, Calabar, once had a king called Essiya, who, like most of the Calabar kings in the olden days, was rich and powerful; but although he was so wealthy, he did not possess many slaves. He therefore used to call upon the animals and birds to help his people with their work. In order to get the work done quickly and well, he determined to appoint head chiefs of all the different species. The elephant he appointed king of the beasts of the forest, and the hippopotamus king of the water animals, until at last it came to the turn of the birds to have their king elected.

Essiya thought for some time which would be the best way to make a good choice, but could not make up his mind, as there were so many different birds who all considered they had claims. There was the hawk with his swift flight, and of hawks there were several species. There were the herons to be considered, and the big spur-winged geese, the hornbill or toucan tribe, and the game birds, such as guinea-fowl, the partridge, and the bustards. Then again, of course, there were all the big crane tribe, who walked about the sandbanks[157] in the dry season, but who disappeared when the river rose, and the big black-and-white fishing eagles. When the king thought of the plover tribe, the sea-birds, including the pelicans, the doves, and the numerous shy birds who live in the forest, all of whom sent in claims, he got so confused, that he decided to have a trial by ordeal of combat, and sent word round the whole country for all the birds to meet the next day and fight it out between themselves, and that the winner should be known as the king bird ever afterwards.

The following morning many thousands of birds came, and there was much screeching and flapping of wings. The hawk tribe soon drove all the small birds away, and harassed the big waders so much, that they very shortly disappeared, followed by the geese, who made much noise, and winged away in a straight line, as if they were playing "Follow my leader." The big forest birds who liked to lead a secluded life very soon got tired of all the noise and bustle, and after a few croaks and other weird noises went home. The game birds had no chance and hid in the bush, so that very

95

soon the only birds left were the hawks and the big black-and-white fishing eagle, who was perched on a tree calmly watching everything. The scavenger hawks were too gorged and lazy to take much interest in the proceedings, and were quietly ignored by the fighting tribe, who were very busy circling and swooping on one another, with much whistling going on. Higher and higher they went, until they disappeared out of sight. Then a few would return to earth, some of them badly torn and with many feathers missing.[158]

At last the fishing eagle said—

"When you have quite finished with this foolishness please tell me, and if any of you fancy yourselves at all, come to me, and I will settle your chances of being elected head chief once and for all;" but when they saw his terrible beak and cruel claws, knowing his great strength and ferocity, they stopped fighting between themselves, and acknowledged the fishing eagle to be their master.

Essiya then declared that Ituen, which was the name of the fishing eagle, was the head chief of all the birds, and should thenceforward be known as the king bird.[13]

From that time to the present day, whenever the young men of the country go to fight they always wear three of the long black-and-white feathers of the king bird in their hair, one on each side and one [159]in the middle, as they are believed to impart much courage and skill to the wearer; and if a young man is not possessed of any of these feathers when he goes out to fight, he is looked upon as a very small boy indeed.

FOOTNOTES

[13]As the king bird is always very difficult to shoot with a bow and arrow, owing to his sharp and keen sight, the young men, when they want his feathers, set traps for him baited with rats, which catch him by the foot in a noose when he seizes them. Except when they are nesting the king birds roost on very high trees, sometimes as many as twenty or thirty on neighbouring trees. They fly many miles from where they get their food, and arrive at their roosting-place just before the sun sets, leaving the next morning at dawn for their favourite haunts. They are very regular in their habits, and you can see them every night at the same time coming from the same direction and flying over the same trees, generally fairly high up in the air. There is a strong belief amongst many natives on the Cross River that the king bird has the power of influencing the luck or the reverse of a canoe. For example, when a trader, having bought a new canoe, is going to market and a king bird crosses the river from right to left, then if he is unlucky at the market that day, whenever the king bird again crosses that particular canoe from right to left he will be unlucky, and the bad luck will stick to the canoe. If, on the other hand, the bird for the first time crosses from left to right, and he is fortunate in his dealings that day at the market, then he will always be lucky in that canoe the day he sees a king bird flying across the river from the left to the right-hand side.

THE END

BY ANDREW LANG

- THE SECRET OF THE TOTEM. 8vo, 10s. 6d. net.
- CUSTOM AND MYTH: Studies of Early Usage and Belief. With 15 Illustrations. Crown 8vo, 3s. 6d.
- MYTH, RITUAL, AND RELIGION. 2 vols. Crown 8vo, 7s.
- MODERN MYTHOLOGY: a Reply to Professor Max Müller. 8vo, 9s.
- MAGIC AND RELIGION. 8vo, 10s. 6d.
- THE MAKING OF RELIGION. Crown 8vo, 5s. net.
- HOMER AND THE EPIC. Crown 8vo, 9s. net.
- HOMER AND HIS AGE. With 8 Illustrations. 8vo, 12s. 6d. net.
- COCK LANE AND COMMON SENSE. Crown 8vo, 3s. 6d.
- THE BOOK OF DREAMS AND GHOSTS. Crown 8vo, 3s. 6d.

LONGMANS, GREEN AND CO.

LONDON, NEW YORK, BOMBAY, AND CALCUTTA